A divine destruction

A divine destruction

by Aamir Ghauri
photographs by Sohail Anjum

Foreword

Dates are remembered for a multitude of reasons. But 8 October, 2005 has a particular resonance. It is a date that millions of Pakistanis and Kashmiris would like to delete from their memory. It is a date that changed the whole course of their lives. While many are trying to rebuild their lives, physical and mental scars are too deep to heal quickly. More importantly, they are hindered in this process by a government whose words are hollow and actions largely invisible.

A Divine Destruction is an attempt to record permanently those moments that destroyed a paradise on earth. But more than that it is an attempt to highlight the plight of the people of Kashmir and northern Pakistan who were told by their rulers that their destruction was an act of God.

It is a visual narration of the public and government response to a devastating and unprecedented natural disaster. The people of Pakistan have had more than their fair share of problems. The October earthquake only added to their long list of miseries. During my trips to the region, survivors told me that they do not like to be referred to as 'lucky to be alive'. They would rather be dead.

Reasons for such fatalism are understandable. Promises of help have failed to materialise; cheques are offered to those who do not have a bank account; monetary compensation is offered at a price. There are thousands of families who have not received a single penny in aid. 'And we do not need one either. We live off nature and if we are told now that nature destroyed us. Fine, that settles the score... doesn't it?' a survivor told me in the Neelum Valley. He lives barely twenty miles from Muzaffarabad, the capital city of Pakistani Kashmir.

Nine months after the earthquake, millions of Kashmiris and Pakistanis remain unaided. Pakistan's requests for international aid remain unanswered as well amid talk of donor fatigue. Nature has not been very kind over the last few years. *Tsunami*, hurricanes, earthquakes – the story keeps growing grimmer.

But then people do ask who was supposed to help them when they need it most, their own government or the international community? Pakistanis now openly question why successive governments, which boast of their nuclear capability, the strength of the military and unparalleled foreign currency reserves, won't take responsibility for helping their own people, rather than relying on the international community for support. But will those in power in Pakistan ever listen to their own people?

Introduction

The area of Pakistani-administered Kashmir is one of the most remote and beautiful on earth. Despite years of unrest over this disputed territory, its people are proud to live in the mountainous, difficult terrain of the Himalayan and Hindukush ranges.

Until, that is, one day in October 2005 when a massive earthquake killed many thousands of people, probably over 100,000, although definite figures are hard to come by. At first, the scale of the damage was hidden, in an area where all communications had been cut.

Once the terrible reality became known, billions of dollars of aid was promised, but more importantly, people from all over the world rushed to help, bringing their skills and goodwill. Medical staff improvised so that they could get on with the urgent job of treating the sick and wounded, many of them children. Simply getting help into these mountainous areas was – and remains – a massive task, one for which the Pakistani government was unprepared.

The photographs in this book tell the unfinished story of the Kashmir earthquake, from the time the news broke to the snows of winter. They show the reality of life for survivors as they searched for their families, for the thousands of children undergoing surgery, for those who mourned loved ones and tried to get back to normal. They document the response of the aid agencies, the military and politicians. But most of all, they show that life does go on, despite everything.

8 October 2005
Earthquake measures 7.6 on Richter scale

8 October, 2005: It was past eight in the morning in Pakistan and Kashmir. The day must have started like any normal day. Millions of men, women and children would have been preparing to go about their business – school children settling down in classrooms after giggling through their assembly formalities; mothers relaxing a while before the mundane worries of cooking, cleaning and washing refilled their brains; office clerks sipping their first round of tea; shopkeepers adjusting their paltry possessions and flapping cotton rags to keep flies away from their merchandise. Life could not have been more normal.

Thousands of them didn't know that they had exhausted their lease of life. Many more were unaware that the next few minutes would change their lives into stories of suffering, sighs and sorrow.

Pakistani military search for survivors in the debris
of Margalla Tower. Getty Images

With Pakistani Kashmir as its nucleus, South Asia was rocked by a mighty earthquake measuring 7.6 on the Richter scale. The tectonic ripples shook the landscape full of mighty mountains and glorious gorges with such ferocity that human dwellings tumbled like autumn leaves.

Pakistan is placed on the confluence of the Eurasian and Indian plates. Earthquakes of mild to major intensity regularly rock parts of the country. Mostly these earthquakes originate in the Hindukush mountain range. People have perished in these tremors without the world knowing about them. But the one that hit the region on 8 October was unprecedented in its ferocity. It was the first killer earthquake with its epicentre in Pakistani Kashmir. The US Geological Survey put that point just north-east of Muzaffarabad in the Neelum Valley. Its ripples, however, were felt as far afield as Kabul in the west and Delhi, some 375 miles to the east.

Kashmir has always been described as a paradise on earth. Its mountains rise to thousands of metres and form part of the majestic Himalayan and Hindukush ranges. Its rivers and streams serpentine through lush green valleys and provide sustenance to millions in India and Pakistan. Kashmiri people are proud inhabitants of one of the most beautiful landscapes on the planet. Feelings are not dissimilar in the adjoining North West Frontier Province (NWFP) of Pakistan. The October earthquake has violently shaken all that for generations.

The devastation of Kashmiri and Frontier towns was known about across the globe within moments, courtesy of Pakistan's burgeoning satellite television networks. Images were few but the live reports by mobile phones from the area told of the horror that was unfolding in the valleys and towns.

For an average television viewer, the earthquake seemed only to have hit Islamabad, the country's capital. Because, for many hours, the flattening of Margalla Tower, a ten-storey block of flats in Islamabad's F-10 Markaz, remained the sole visual image of the tragedy. Over a hundred people perished in the collapse. Margalla Tower was known as one of the best addresses in Islamabad where government officials, business people and high-paid foreigners lived. One of them was Maay Fairs, a diminutive Iraqi with bright blonde highlights in her hair.

Imagining what happened to Fairs, Susanne Koeble of *Spiegel Online* wrote: *'(Maay Fairs) had just placed the breakfast dishes on the table for her children and husband, a United Nations worker, when the earth started to shake. It was just before 9am local time. Fairs grabbed her youngest child, two-year-old Abbas. The eight floors of her apartment building came crashing down on top of her, as if a mountain had slid into the valley. Afterwards it was pitch black and silent.'*

Fairs and Abbas survived for 63 hours under the rubble before they were pulled out alive by the British rescuers who formed part of the first foreign team to reach Pakistan to help. Fairs was found in a small cavity, her legs trapped and her small child held firmly against her belly. Her husband and second son were not so lucky – they didn't survive. Many residents jumped to their deaths when the top floors started crashing down. The falling rubble crushed their already broken bodies.

The tower's collapse brutally revealed the paucity of essential public services in Pakistan's 'modern' capital. Images of soldiers desperately trying to separate concrete from iron with their bare hands showed the limits of the relief operation that was under way at the tragic site. In Pakistan, many believe that people like Maay Fairs survived only through the expertise and technical capability of the foreign rescue teams. The Islamabad police chief appealed to private construction firms to lend heavy equipment to remove the debris. If that was the case in the federal capital, one can only imagine what might have happened in the distant villages in the mountains further north.

While the meagre rescue effort was struggling at the site, the government resorted to cosmetic posturing; issuing orders to arrest those responsible for using substandard building materials; apprehending those who allowed the passage of a faulty building design and so on – all typical Pakistani bureaucratic shenanigans. With escalating media demands for an honest appraisal of the scale of the earthquake, government spokesmen employed dubious tactics to repel pressure. Some government officials described the collapse of Margalla Tower as 'God's will' as it was the only block of flats to have tumbled out of many.

President General Pervez Musharraf changed his khaki uniform for a commando outfit and visited the demolished site to oversee the rescue operations. He described the catastrophe as a testing time for himself, the government and the nation. Similar tactics were later used by many of his ministers who visited F-10 with heavy police escorts to see for themselves the crumbled building. People described these trips as mere photo-opportunities.

Like all natural disasters of such proportions, no one could precisely predict the scale of devastation. What, however, doubled the shock for the Pakistani nation was the casual nonchalance of some of the Pakistani ministers. A few of them, in fact, even advised the inquisitive media not to worry as nothing of consequence had happened. The federal information minister reportedly said that only a few thousand people had died and life in the quake-hit areas went on as normal. Dr Omar Ayub, the president of the Pakistan Medical Association, spoke for the majority of Pakistanis when he described the minister's remarks as 'shameful'.

References to 'destiny' also came from senior military officers who started to take control of the rescue and relief work in quake-hit areas. *'Those destined to die in the quake have died and there's nothing anyone can do about it,'* a military officer involved in relief operations told the BBC. But he was somehow sure that *'not a single survivor would die of cold or hunger'*.

Pakistani governments – military or civilian – have a habit of concealing facts. At a time when panic was spreading like pain in a seriously bruised nervous system, the official line was 'all okay and under control'. The need to know the facts, being demanded so loudly, was not really catered for in the government structure. Its' denial left many Pakistanis reeling with anger. It also hindered the requisite response from the rest of the world. How could you get a sympathetic international response when important Pakistani ministers were claiming that nothing had happened?

Pakistani President General Pervez Musharraf speaks to earthquake victims in Muzaffarabad, capital city of Pakistani-administered Kashmir. Getty Images

Crushed cars underneath the collapsed Margalla Tower. Getty Images

While the government was too slow to respond, the media – national and international – made the earthquake an international story. By 10 October, news pages and top-of-the-hour bulletins across the world were telling the tragic tales. In one of his first reports, Declan Walsh of *The Guardian* described the destruction of Pakistani Kashmir as:

'Muzaffarabad… has become a city of fear and mourning. The quake turned streets into grey mountains of collapsed concrete, twisted metal and crushed cars. Power lines were strewn across roads, their asphalt surfaces split, and two small trucks hung from a tree, apparently flung from the crest of a nearby hill. The toll remains provisional – hundreds, probably thousands, of bodies lie beneath the rubble, buried beyond the reach of the only rescue tools available, sledgehammers and human hands. As darkness fell, the city's population huddled by lamplight outside their destroyed homes and shops, terrified to sleep under a roof again. A snaking ribbon of headlights lit up the road to Mansehra, 33 miles away, as thousands of residents fled by car, rickshaw or on foot.'

The infrastructural damage was massive but such a loss could be remedied. It was the loss of human life that haunted the city. It was a disaster that did not differentiate between young and old, men or women, rich or poor. Children were, in fact, the most affected. Mohammad Waseem, a Muzaffarabad schoolboy told his story to CNN's Mathew Chance:

'We were taking our exams when the whole (school) building started to shake and collapse… I think a few (students) on the ground floor scrambled out. But the students on the upper floors all died… We were all hoping to be engineers or doctors, but now we can't even think about our futures. We have nothing left.'

The Kashmiri Prime Minister Sardar Sikandar Hayat Khan likened himself to a keeper of a graveyard. His offices had been housed in one of the worst hit buildings and now government affairs were being run from a tent. Government buildings – hospitals, colleges, universities, police stations – all were reduced to rubble, raising serious questions about the quality of their construction.

Balakot and Bagh were the other worst hit towns. The destruction of historic Balakot was powerfully portrayed by *The Guardian*:

'Balakot looks like a town that has been eaten alive. The convulsion buckled the earth, chewed up buses and levelled practically every building in sight. Nobody can provide the death toll because there is nobody to ask. The mayor, the police chief, the magistrate – all swallowed up by the earth.'

Images of men, women and children making a beeline to relief camps became a routine in the press. Thousands of victims who were lucky to be alive and well enough to walk left their demolished homes for tented towns that have sprung up all over Kashmir and northern Pakistan. Those who came to save the injured ended up digging out the dead.

The tragedy was followed by a bigger trauma. How to respond to this unprecedented natural disaster in the country's history? Pakistan had had floods and Kashmir had quivered in the past, but not to this magnitude. But since Pakistan, like many a time in the past, is suffering from a quasi-military government, the civilian arm of the government failed to take effective and decisive steps in this situation.

Whatever rescue work was going on, it was obscured by confusion. The president had a five-point programme for rescue and relief while the prime minister announced a twelve-point plan. It was impossible for the civilian spokesmen of the government to inform the public about the true nature and extent of the disaster. With Kashmir being one of the main theatres of devastation, the army was overly nervous about giving the media access to the strategically sensitive areas. Despite this, reports filtered through describing the wiping out of villages and deaths of hundreds of Pakistani Army soldiers posted on the Line of Control between Pakistan and India.

These reports were helpful and alarming at the same time. Commenting on the media's role, the *Herald* wrote: *'At least two aspects of the media coverage of the earthquake rubbed the Musharraf government the wrong way. First, it made it evident to the people at large that the army did not have a built-*

A survivor receives the key for a one-room house from Pakistani TV celebrity, Tariq Aziz. Within the disaster-hit areas over a hundred such houses were built and donated by UK-based charity Helping Hands.

in capacity to respond quickly to unforeseen natural calamities, especially in a disputed area such as Kashmir where security concerns take precedence over those of human welfare. Secondly, it touched on the alternative view that the disaster could have been better managed had a strong system of local administration existed in the affected areas.'

The government response was splattered all over the place. Statements were too many – 'from knee jerk reaction to utopian' – action was too little. The setting up of new rescue and relief bodies was the first step. General Musharraf established the President's Relief Fund, netting about six billion rupees (approximately £60 million) within a few days, while Prime Minister Shaukat Aziz initiated a relief package of one billion rupees (approximately £10 million) for the victims of the disaster.

A national Earthquake Reconstruction and Rehabilitation Authority (ERRA) was also created. The need for the government to spearhead these bodies showed the complete and utter failure of the existing departments and proved that government and delegation in Pakistan could not go beyond the usual bureaucratic stagnation.

Those military officers who were put in charge of the rescue and relief effort proved to be over-confident of their abilities and capabilities. A military officer told the *BBC News*: *'They [foreign relief agencies] came here treating us the same way as they would treat warlords or private militias in some African countries… but within a couple of weeks, they were not willing to work with anyone but us.'*

What, in fact, the military officer could not have said was that there exists no-one else to talk to. Civilian government departments have eroded a long time ago. Government hospitals remain hollow structures with scant medical facilities. Necessities like ambulances, X-ray machines and scanning facilities exist only on paper. Many hospitals and basic medical health units do not have essential staff. The Public Works Department (PWD) used to be a half-effective outfit in towns like Bagh, Balakot and Abbotabad. Not any more.

Not everything was wrong with the military's involvement in the reconstruction and rehabilitation effort. It was the military leadership not the soldiers who faltered on many fronts during this testing time. Writing for *The Nation*, Hussain Haqqani commented: *'One must acknowledge the dedication of army aviation helicopter pilots for running humanitarian sorties notwithstanding exhaustion and bad weather. Hard-working officers and army jawans have made an immense contribution in digging out the dead and helping survivors.'*

The same could be said about the army's engineering corps. It was their work of clearing thousands of tonnes of debris blocking the road network or creating 'jeepable' tracks within days of the earthquake that allowed relief agencies like the World Food Program (WFP) and International Committee of Red Cross (ICRC) to reach distant areas in Kashmir and the NWFP.

While government response remained questionable, the public reaction in Pakistan was remarkable. The sheer size of the public mobilisation was unparalleled in the country's history – not matched even during the 1965 Indo-Pakistani war or the calamitous cyclone that hit the former East Pakistan in 1970.

A volunteer army of Pakistani men took matters into their own hands. From 9 October onwards, the twisting mountain tracks leading to quake-affected areas were clogged with cars, trucks and buses. These volunteers came from as near as the next villages and as far as Detroit and Michigan. They came from all walks of life – labourers, office clerks, university professors, engineers, doctors – bringing modest supplies of medicine and food but abundant promises to help. They said it was their duty to come and do whatever they could.

Doctors from all over the country drove to the worst-hit areas, setting up operating theatres wherever they could. They carried out hundreds of operations every day.

A landslide brought down the entire side of a mountain during the earthquake. Panos Pictures

BT set up four communication sites in Athmukam where surviviors were able to make free calls.

'Most of these operations were amputations. In most cases we did not have options. It was either limbs or lives and we had to choose the latter,' said Dr Saad Ghauri, an orthopaedic surgeon, who left his job in Lahore to be in Abbotabad. 'The government hospital building was declared unsafe due to serious structural damage so all the patients were moved into tents erected on the lawns of the hospital. The air reeked of antiseptics.'

International public and private response was also commendable. Ordinary people, small businesses and large corporations did whatever they could to help the victims. Millions were raised through telethons across Asia, Europe and North America. On one hand children donated their pocket money, while on the other telecommunication giants like BT spent £3 million to help establish four communication sites, one each at Rawalpindi, Athmukam, Chinari and Chakothi so people could finally contact relatives or seek help from the relief agencies.

I arrived in Kasmir a few weeks after the quake. While driving from Islamabad to Muzzafarabad, I reminisced about my various trips to Kashmir, full of beautiful memories. A lunch at Domail – where the Jhelum and Neelum rivers meet; cascading streams hurrying to join these rivers; shaking and swinging footbridges that connect valleys; winding roads along the rebellious rivers; roadside tea kiosks for stop-sip-and-go journey breaks; shingle tracks that took me to the picturesque Leepa Valley just yards from the Line of Control where Pakistani and Indian soldiers sit all year long in trenches eyeball to eyeball.

These images were brutally shattered by the reality that awaited me in Kashmir. Houses on hilltops were turned into grit and valleys were full of tent villages. International charities, Muslim relief organisations, Islamist political parties and groups fighting for Kashmiri liberation from the Indian occupation – all were running camps, many a time side by side, for the earthquake victims.

The major part of Muzaffarabad city presented a perplexing picture. There were rows of shack-like shops in bazaars completely untouched by the tremor, while others were replaced by stones and boulders thrust many metres forwards by the mighty mountain movement of the earth's surface. The town's old fort that must have withstood many a battle, had now crumbled like a sandcastle – its walls cracked and parapets tumbled down. The mountains overlooking the city were sliced like cake – coming down in tonnes of powdery mash to block the Neelum River. The army had to detonate these artificial dams in order to resume the water flow.

People wandered aimlessly. Their faces were drawn and hearts full of pain. They were desperate for help but wouldn't ask. Those I spoke to told me they couldn't admit to losing their self-respect. 'This is all we are left with'. When questioned as to what happened to government aid, they would respond 'what government?' or: 'The government is one of the fatalities of the earthquake. There is no one to talk to, nowhere to go to seek help.'

Newspapers and media reports were full of warnings and promises. Warnings by the international organisations like the United Nations and the ICRC of worse to come when winter hits the region. Jan Egeland, UN's relief chief, had already admitted that the earthquake was the worst logistical nightmare for his organisation. 'We thought the *tsunami* was the worst we could get. This is worse.' He wanted international effort to airlift victims trapped in the remotest parts of the disaster area to safer places.

The UN was also critical of the lack of aid from the richer countries. Its aid co-ordinator Andrew McLeod said that the major donors were going to have to look themselves in the mirror and ask why. His reference was to the estimation by various relief agencies that people remained without any aid weeks after the earthquake. Secretary General Kofi Annan warned of a second wave of deaths if the international aid pledges did not materialise in time.

For its part, the Pakistani government was making utopian promises. The aid that had not arrived was to be equitably distributed among the victims encamped in the open all over the place. The death toll rose to over 85,000 and millions were homeless. Many claimed that the government was all talk, but that is what governments in Pakistan have been good at since its inception in 1947.

En route to Chakothi, I stopped at what once were human dwellings. People were busy raising thatched huts. Many were using the roofs of their demolished houses as floors for the new homes. 'It was my home where I lived with my parents and children. Now it is the grave of four of them,' Fazaldad, who worked in Muzaffarabad as a casual labourer, told me. He could not wait for reconstruction and rehabilitation teams to help. Others told me that the only government help they received in a month were three tents dropped by helicopters:

'We are over 70 families living here as a block and we are not very far from the main road'. So were they angry at the lack of help coming to them?

'Not at all. Governments have done nothing for us in the past and we do not expect them to do anything different this time round. God is with us and we will survive.'

They were hospitable and would not let me leave without having dinner with them. I felt ashamed but was told that by tradition they could not let a guest go without having a meal. I wished that the governors of this beautiful land were half as courageous, honest and straightforward.

The situation in and around Balakot was too grim to describe. The town looked crumbled as if stepped on by a giant:

'Shattered homes, shocked faces, scattered people, stony eyes, toppled tombstones and desolation everywhere. Anyway....Eid greetings' – that is one of the text messages people in these towns were sending each other when the Muslim holy month of Ramadan culminated. The epicentre of the quake might be closer to Muzaffarabad but Balakot, it seemed, took the brunt of it. The town seemed a prehistoric wreck where people were trying, without hope, to find their loved ones.

By the end of November, the Pakistani government was losing patience with the slow speed of international aid. Though the nation and people were thankful to countries like Britain, France, Germany, China and United Arab Emirates for sending rescue teams within hours of the earthquake, the relief contributions were not as swift as Islamabad would have liked.

The editorials continually compared the swiftness and enormity of international aid after the South East Asian tsunami with the slackness and paucity of donations being experienced after the Pakistani earthquake. Then there were those who criticised the richer nations rather diplomatically by pointing out the

A man stands outside his temporary one-room house, built and donated by Islamic Relief, a UK-based charity.

possibility of 'donor fatigue'. Those affected, however, might have judged there to be more energy spent on words than on actions to relieve their plight.

Desperate for international money to carry out relief operations, Pakistan called for an international donors' conference in Islamabad on 19 November. Pressured by the severe and sustained criticism from the Pakistani president and the heads of international organisations, over 80 countries and international agencies attended the conference. It was the largest ever international gathering held in Pakistan. Countries from all regions of the world came to Islamabad.

The conference was meant to share the findings of the assessment study with Pakistan's development partners, present the government's reconstruction and rehabilitation strategy and seek international community's financial, technical and in-kind support towards meeting the costs of the rehabilitation and reconstruction in the earthquake-affected zone.

The assessment itself had been prepared by the Asian Development Bank and the World Bank, along with experts from other international organisations. These included the British Department for International Development (DFID), the German Agency for Technical Cooperation (GTZ), German banking group KfW, Japan Bank for International Cooperation (JBIC), Japan International Cooperation Agency (JICA), United States Agency for International Development (USAID), World Health Organization (WHO), UN Food and Agriculture Organization (FAO) and UN Children's Fund (UNICEF). The United Nations Development Programme carried out detailed surveys between 24 October and 5 November with the aim of providing decision-makers and stakeholders with a quantitative basis upon which to design a comprehensive reconstruction strategy.

It was estimated that Pakistan needed around six billion dollars to rehabilitate the people and areas affected by the earthquake. The donors' conference pledged 6.189 billion dollars. But of much to the consternation to the Musharraf government, only a small portion of these pledges were to be realised in real terms. Almost 75 percent of these pledges were offered as a loan. Similarly, a large part of the over 2.2 billion dollars that came in grants was also kept away from the government.

Three men sit on a cracked road outside Balakot to discuss and share their losses in the earthquake. Many in Kashmir and northern Pakistan remain in shock about how their lives have been turned upside down in a matter of minutes.

People on the street were asking questions as to why the international community had such a high level of mistrust in the government of Pakistan. The international aid agencies were adamant about working through their local partners, albeit in tandem with the Pakistani government and the army. Similarly, most of the foreign monies were released by countries to organisations registered with them. There was such mistrust of the Pakistan's quasi-military government that international pressure forced a change at the top of ERRA. Within months of his appointment as the head of the newly-created Pakistani agency for reconstruction and rehabilitation, Lieutenant General Mohammad Zubair was replaced by a civilian. The Pakistani press reported that the demand for change came from the multilateral and bilateral donors who had pledged billions of dollars for earthquake relief. It is interesting that at the time of his appointment General Zubair had been described as the 'most appropriate man' for the job by General Musharraf.

While political issues mushroomed around the rescue, relief and rehabilitation operation, a bevy of international personalities visited the devastated areas – including presidents, prime ministers, princes and princesses, politicians, Hollywood celebrities and, of course, the international paparazzi. They would meet President Musharraf or Prime Minister Aziz, talk to the press, visit refugee camps, converse with victims, pose for photographs with women and children, play cricket with boys – all good public relations. But what did the people gain? Mostly nothing at all and what little did arrive reached only very few.

When I visited Kashmir again in January 2006, the stories of the victims' distress had multiplied. The government's relief packages were a sham. People were being asked to pay bribes to receive the compensation cheques, which were largely useless as most of these people have no bank account. What could they do with a cheque even if lucky enough to receive one? The allocation of money was also chaotic. Many of those living close to larger towns were not given any compensation because 'they couldn't prove their ownership of properties destroyed in the earthquake'. The government must have known better than anyone else that these people never had title deeds to their properties. They had been living in the mountains for generations, long before there was a country called Pakistan.

My third trip to these unfortunate areas was in March 2006. The government had moved on with its agenda. Promises were still being made – of new earthquake-proof houses, of means of livelihood, of infrastructure, of a better life.

Now the people here are beginning to find their equilibrium again. They can laugh at the hypocrisy: 'Why would the governments give us all that now, when they have never given us anything in the past? They love making promises but we know that promises are meant to be broken. We know that.'

These were the words of Mohammad Akram, who once ran a pharmacy. Like thousands of victims of the October earthquake, he just wanders around looking for a job.

The trauma of the worst natural disaster in the country's history will remain imprinted on the minds of millions of Pakistanis as long as they live. But they talk of other lessons they have learnt in this sad chapter. Pakistan's *Herald* magazine spoke for most of the people in its December 2005 edition:

'The Pakistani nation has always been alive to collective challenges but leaders who could channelise the energy of spontaneous mobilisation such as the one we saw following the October 8 quake have been few and far between. And as these developments show, General Musharraf is clearly not one of them.'

For many the paradise they knew has indeed been lost. The days will no longer start as they did before 8 October, 2005. They have survived – but for many, homes, livelihood, families, and dreams collapsed in a single shattering moment.

While political mayhem seems unlikely to allow the full percolation of the support they deserve as they struggle to meet each difficult new day, their courage and resilience will take more than an earthquake to shatter.

Residents carry relief supplies amidst a scene of devastation in Balakot. Panos Pictures

Next page: A body lies where a thriving market once stood. Panos Pictures

The immediate tragedy was followed by a bigger trauma. Just how would governments and people respond to this unprecedented natural disaster?

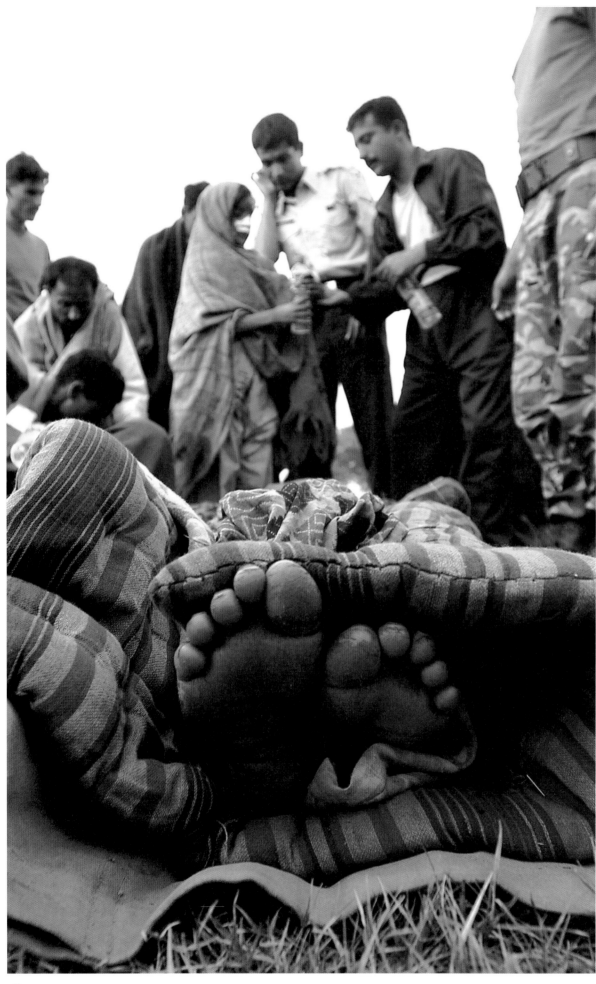

Previous page: The destruction of Balakot Sohail Anjum

Left: A severely injured person lies wrapped in a blanket after being flown by helicopter to Chaklala military air base from a destroyed Kashmiri village. Panos Pictures

Above: The once bustling streets of the northern town of Balakot look more like a rubbish dump after the earthquake. Sohail Anjum

Above: A man digs for any valuable articles underneath the debris of a demolished building in Balakot. Sohail Anjum

Far right: A victim lies under the rubble of collapsed buildings in Balakot in the North West Frontier Province. Getty Images

Far top right: The hand of a victim emerges from the debris of the Margalla Tower. Getty Images

Far bottom: A father looks at the face of his dead child at Balakot two days after the disaster. Life will never be the same again. Getty Images

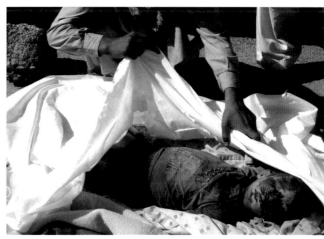

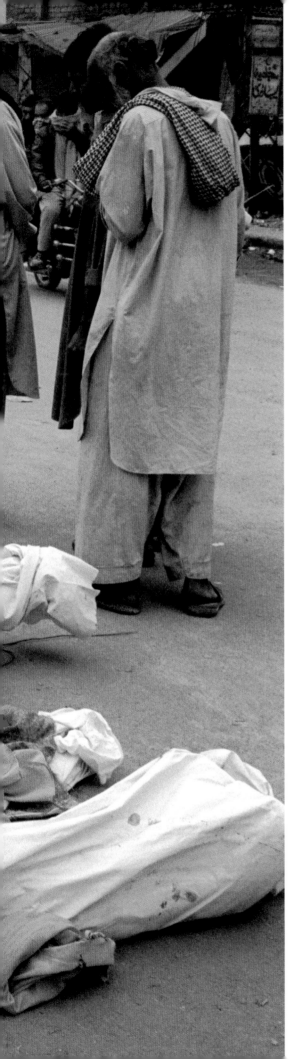

Bodies are placed on the road for identification.
Panos Pictures

The convulsion buckled the earth... and levelled practically everything in sight.

Quake survivors cross a damaged bridge on the Jhelum River in Ghari Dupatta, some 10 miles south of Muzaffarabad. Getty Images

Two survivors on a damaged bridge outside a Kashmiri
town in the Neelum Valley, near Muzaffarabad, the capital
of Pakistani administered Kashmir. Getty Images

Kashmiri earthquake survivors cross over the Neelum River
using a damaged bridge near Muzaffarabad. Getty Images

A partially damaged bridge still provides a valuable link for aid to come through. Panos Pictures

People walk past overturned vehicles in Balakot,
a day after the earthquake. Getty Images

Initially, the only images were of the capital, Islamabad. No-one outside the region could see the total devastation which had hit Kashmir.

Previous page: The minaret of a mosque is now part of the rubble littered all over Kashmir. Panos Pictures

Left: The infrastructure of this remote region is badly affected, leaving many villages accessible only by air. Panos Pictures

Above: Damaged infrastructure: A cracked road in the destroyed town of Balakot. Sohail Anjum

Survivors carry their belongings as they evacuate the area near Chakothi, close to the Line of Control between Pakistan and India. Getty Images

Previous page: A partially destroyed memorial in Balakot. Sohail Anjum

Left: Government offices reduced to rubble in Bagh. Sohail Anjum

People sit on top of a destroyed building in Balakot. Sohail Anjum

Left: The remains of a shop destroyed by the earthquake in Balakot. *Sohail Anjum*

Right: Nothing was immune to the earthquake's destructive force. *Sohail Anjum*

Previous page: A vehicle is crushed under the roof that once provided it with shelter. Sohail Anjum

Above: A row of partially destroyed shops in one of Balakot's main bazaars. Sohail Anjum

'Shattered homes, shocked faces, scattered people, stony eyes, toppled tombstones and desolation everywhere. Anyway… Eid greetings.'

Mobile phone message

Left: Friday prayers are being offered on 28 October, 2005 at the Jamia Hamam Wali mosque in Muzaffarabad. Getty Images

Above: Men praying in front of a collapsed mosque in the town of Balakot. Sohail Anjum

Previous page: Young Kashmiri survivors hold lamps during a ceremony in celebration of 'World Children's Day' stressing that child victims of the 8 October earthquake would require sustained support to enable their recovery. Getty Images

Above: Pakistani earthquake survivors offer noon prayers. Smaller aftershocks continued to be felt in the area over the following months but the damage had already been done. Getty Images

Previous page: Prayers are an important part of everyday life as people attempt to get back to normal in the devastated town of Balakot. Getty Images

Above: A special prayer on Eid-ul-Fitr – an emotional day as people try to come to terms with the deaths of family members. Getty Images

Pakistan needs some six billion dollars for the aid effort. Despite tremendous efforts by a number of countries, many others have yet to turn their pledges into reality.

American Chinook helicopters and other aircraft from the Pakistani and foreign air forces transporting injured people. Around 130 sorties were made in one day from Chaklala military air base in Rawalpindi. Panos Pictures

Previous page: A US Chinook helicopter loaded with relief supplies flies into Muzaffarabad. Sohail Anjum

Above: A UN pilot approaches a landing strip already crowded with US Chinook helicopters loaded with relief supplies. Getty Images

Above: US navy workers unload a truck from the USS Pearl Harbor at Karachi Port. The USS Pearl Harbor brought 140 tons of heavy equipment, including trucks to carry relief supplies and earth-moving equipment. Getty Images

Above right: A US Marine posing at Muzaffarabad airport. Sohail Anjum

Mohammad Ashfaq (R) of the British charity, Helping Hands Worldwide visits a relief camp in Abottabad, one of many that the charity set up in Kashmir and northern Pakistan to help victims. Sohail Anjum

Previous page: Displaced and homeless women push for the aid
being delivered by trucks. Panos Pictures

Above: Pakistani-American army medical officer, Tabassum, talks
to his colleague, O'Neal, at the US Mobile Army Surgical Hospital
in Muzaffarabad. Sohail Anjum

Far right: US army medical staff clean-up after a day of activity
at the US Mobile Army Surgical Hospital. Sohail Anjum

US and Pakistani flags fly at the US Mobile Army Surgical Hospital in Muzaffarabad. Sohail Anjum

Next page: Four weeks after the earthquake, a decomposed body is found in an erstwhile market place in Balakot. Sohail Anjum

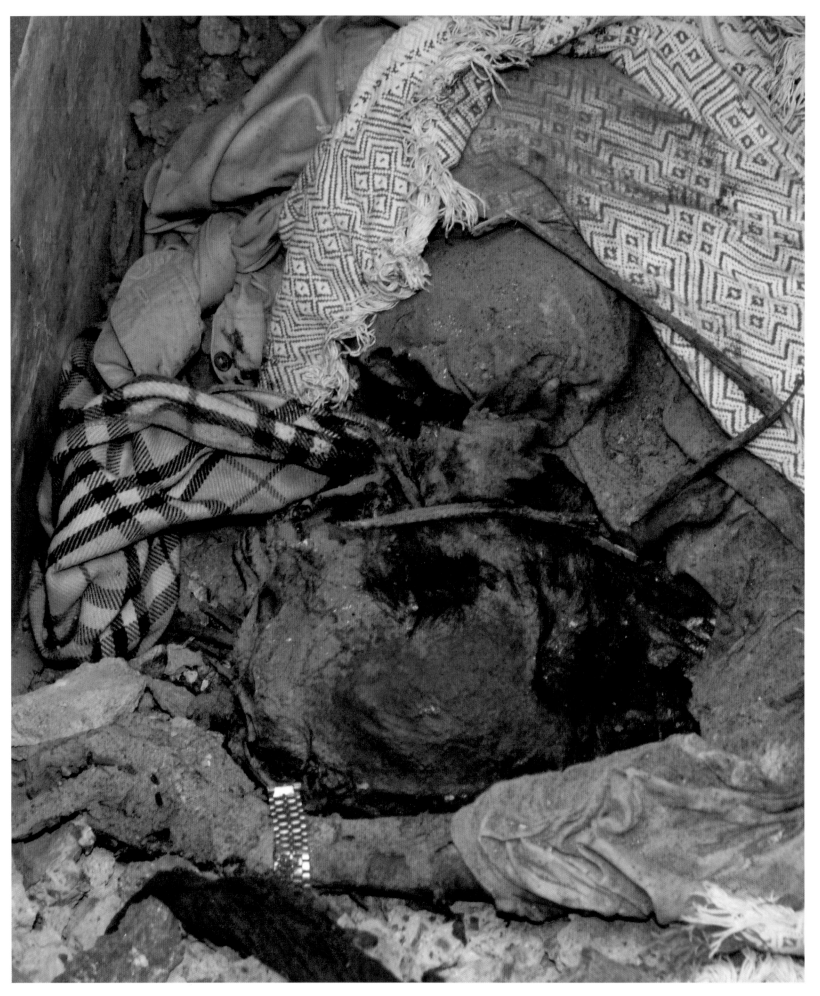

Doctors from all over the country and abroad rushed to the worst-hit areas, setting up operating theatres where they could and performing hundreds of operations in a day.

A Kashmiri child recovering from serious injuries at a relief camp in the grounds of the Ayub Medical College Hospital in Abbotabad. Sohail Anjum

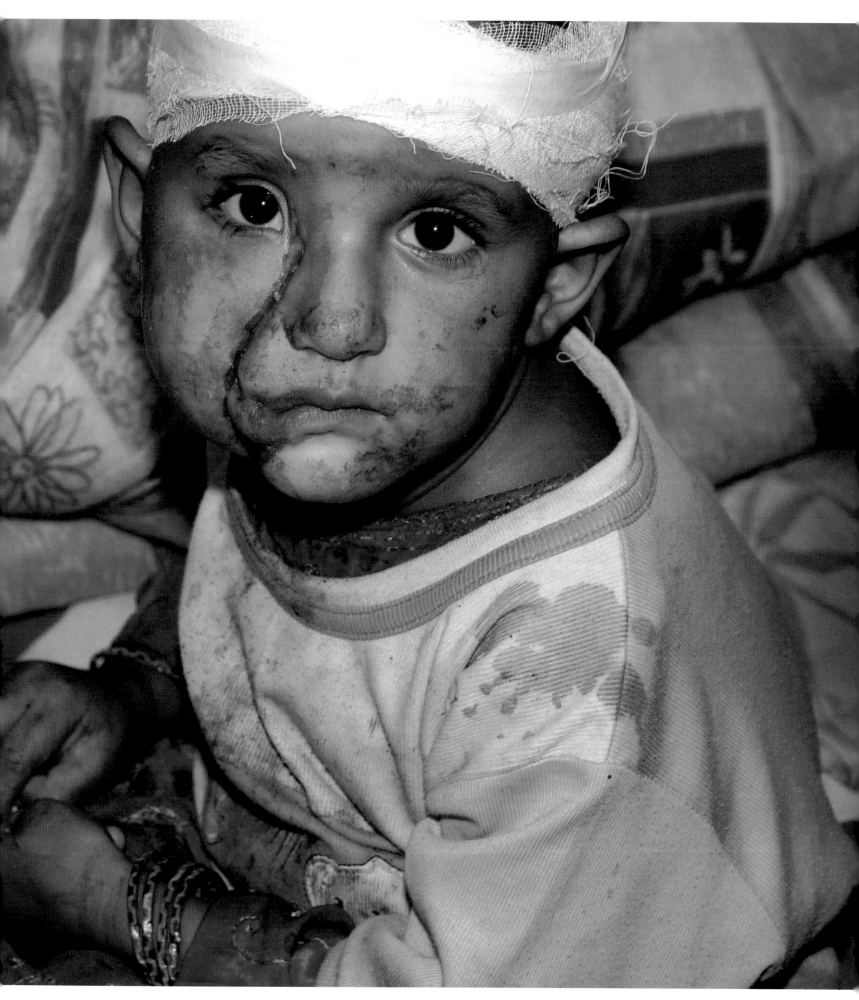

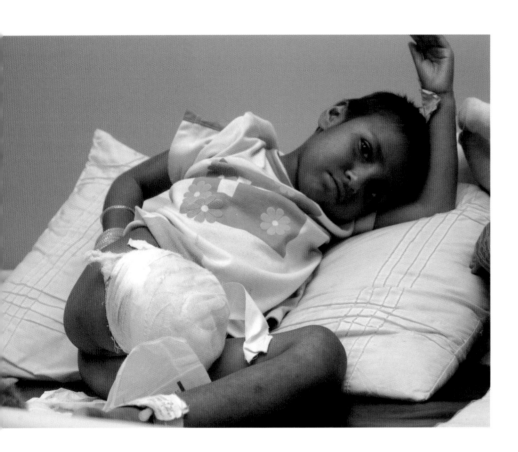

Above: A young girl recovers after having her right leg amputated at the Pakistan Institute of Medical Sciences (PIMS) in Islamabad. Sohail Anjum

Far right: A smiling young boy plays in the corridor of the children's ward of the Pakistan Institute of Medical Sciences after receiving treatment for his head injuries. Sohail Anjum

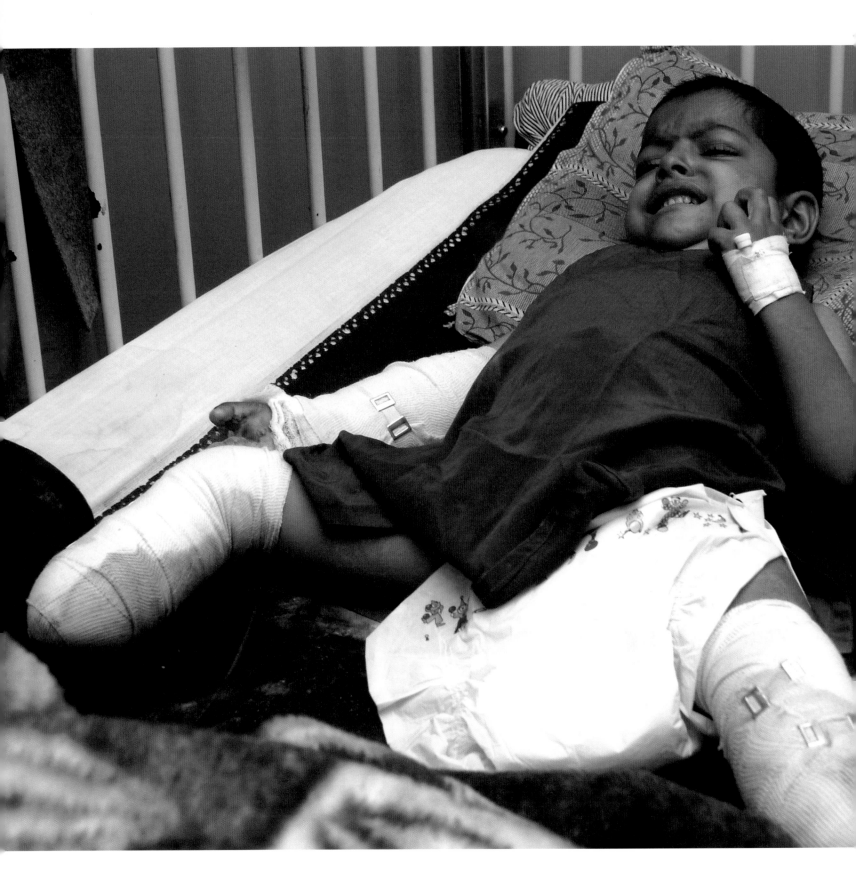

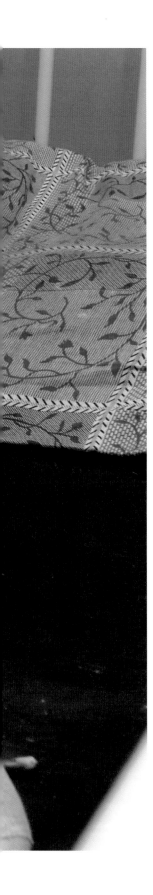

A young girl cries out in pain following a double leg amputation at the Pakistan Institute of Medical Sciences. Sohail Anjum

A young boy leaves the operation theatre after hours of operating to pin his multiple fractures at the Pakistan Institute of Medical Sciences. Sohail Anjum

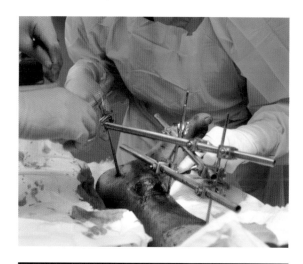

Top: A team of volunteer British doctors carry out a bone operation on a survivor of the earthquake at Al-Shifa Hospital in Rawalpindi. Sohail Anjum

Below: A volunteer British doctor is busy in a skin graft operation on an earthquake victim in a Rawalpindi hospital. Sohail Anjum

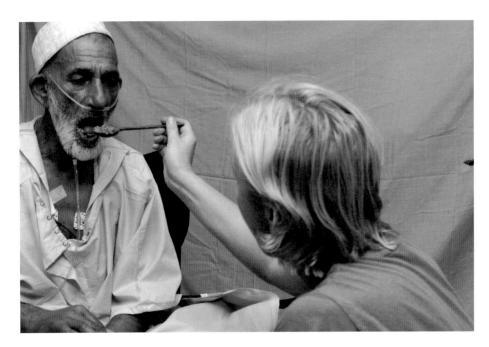

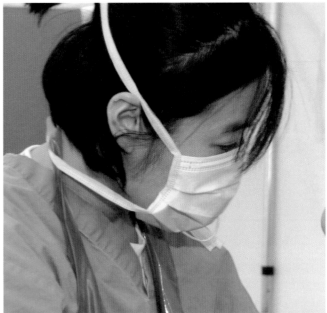

Above: A patient being spoon fed by a member of the army medical staff at the US Army Mobile Army Surgical Hospital. Sohail Anjum

Across: Members of the Korean Medical Team from Seoul Asan Hospital tending to a patient in a special tent set up by KUMC Medical Disaster for Pakistan, in Abbotabad. Sohail Anjum

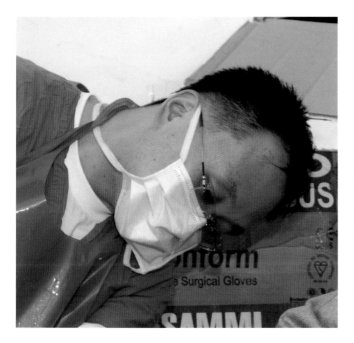
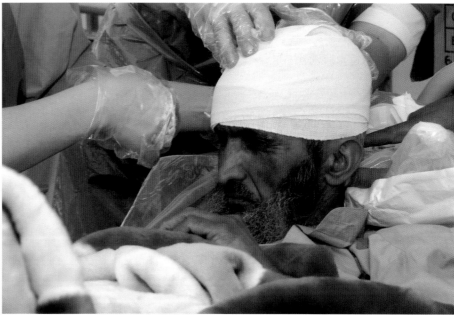

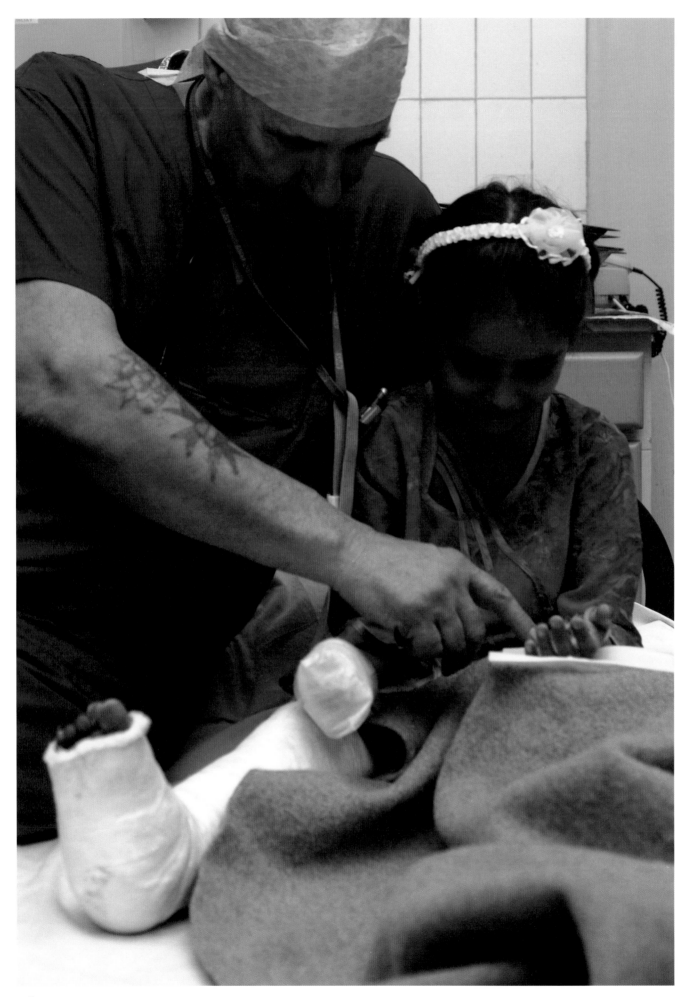

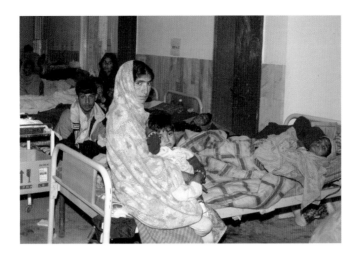

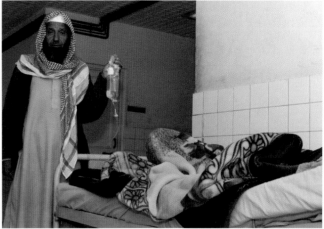

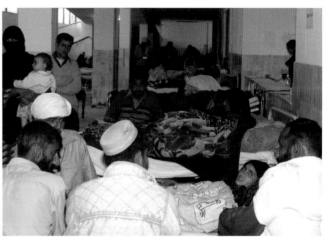

Far left: A volunteer British doctor shares a moment with a young patient at Al-Shifa Hospital. Sohail Anjum

Top left: Relatives of the injured wait with their loved ones at a hospital in Muzaffarabad. Sohail Anjum

Top right: An elderly man attends to his wife as she waits to receive medical attention at the Ayub Medical College Hospital, Abbottabad. Sohail Anjum

Bottom right: Hospital corridors offer refuge once the wards and rooms are full. Sohail Anjum

Kind words: A volunteer doctor talks to an elderly survivor, one of many who were brought to Al-Shifa Hospital for medical help. Sohail Anjum

Next page: A young girl with serious head injuries poses for the camera after receiving medical treatment in the children's ward at the Pakistan Institute of Medical Sciences. Sohail Anjum

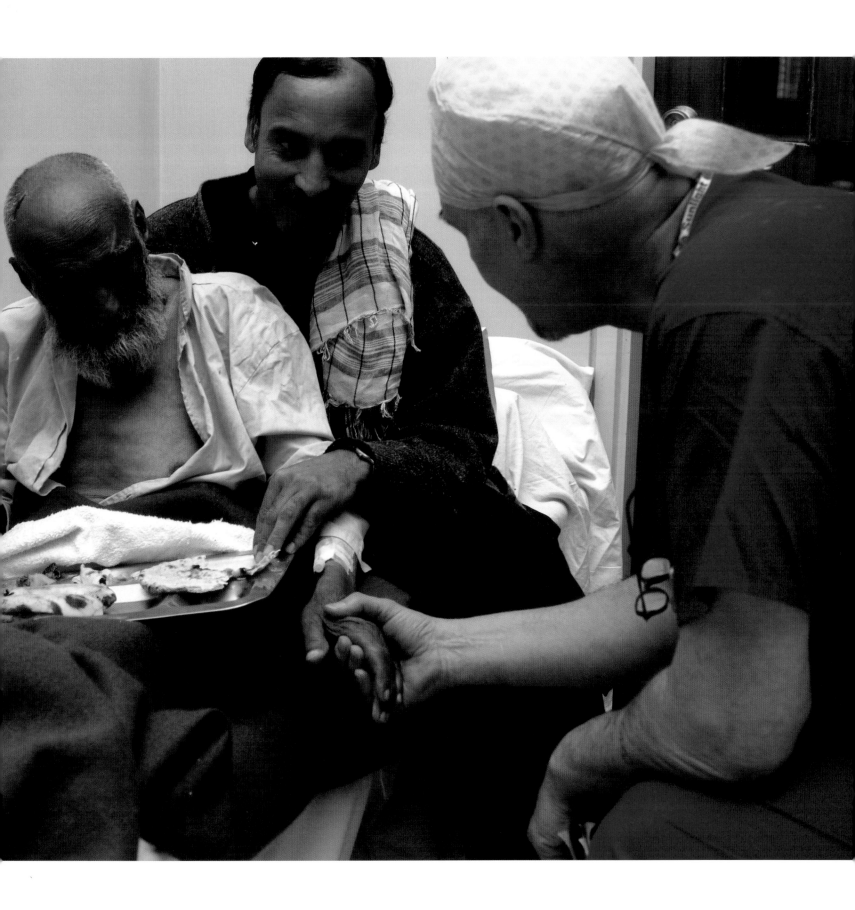

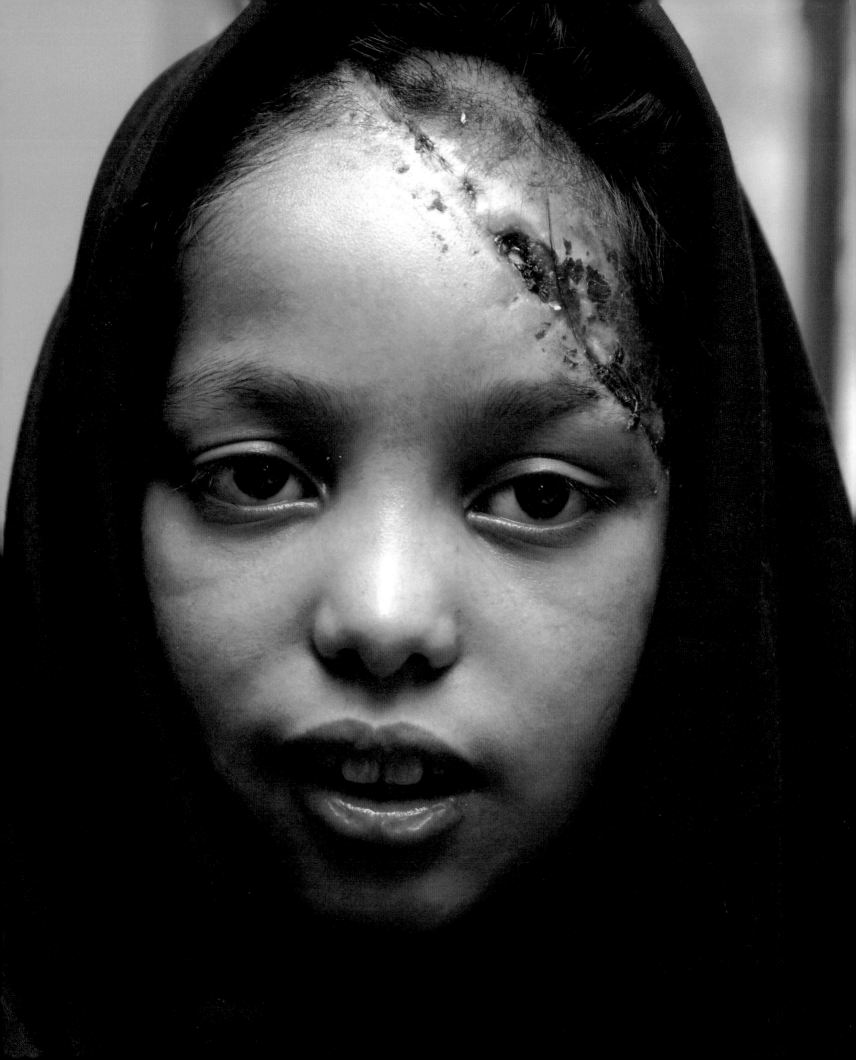

Most operations were amputations. In most cases, surgeons were forced to choose between lives and limbs. They chose the latter...

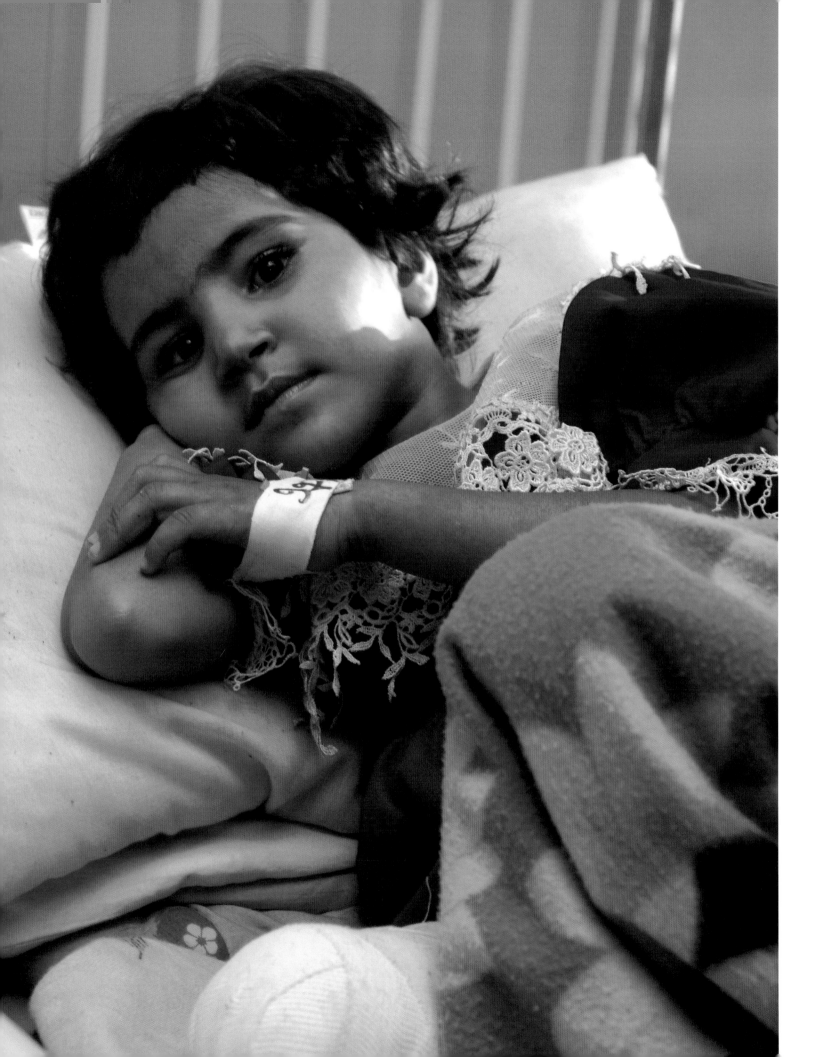

Left: A young girl recovering from a leg amputation at the Pakistan Institute of Medical Sciences in Islamabad. Sohail Anjum

Right: A young girl recovering from a leg amputation is carried by her mother at the Pakistan Institute of Medical Sciences. Sohail Anjum

Below right: The Combined Military Hospital in Rawalpindi was faced with dealing with many horrific injuries sustained by young children. Sohail Anjum

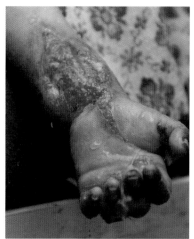

Eleven-year-old Kursheed lies in bed after having his left arm amputated at the Pakistan Institute of Medical Sciences. Sohail Anjum

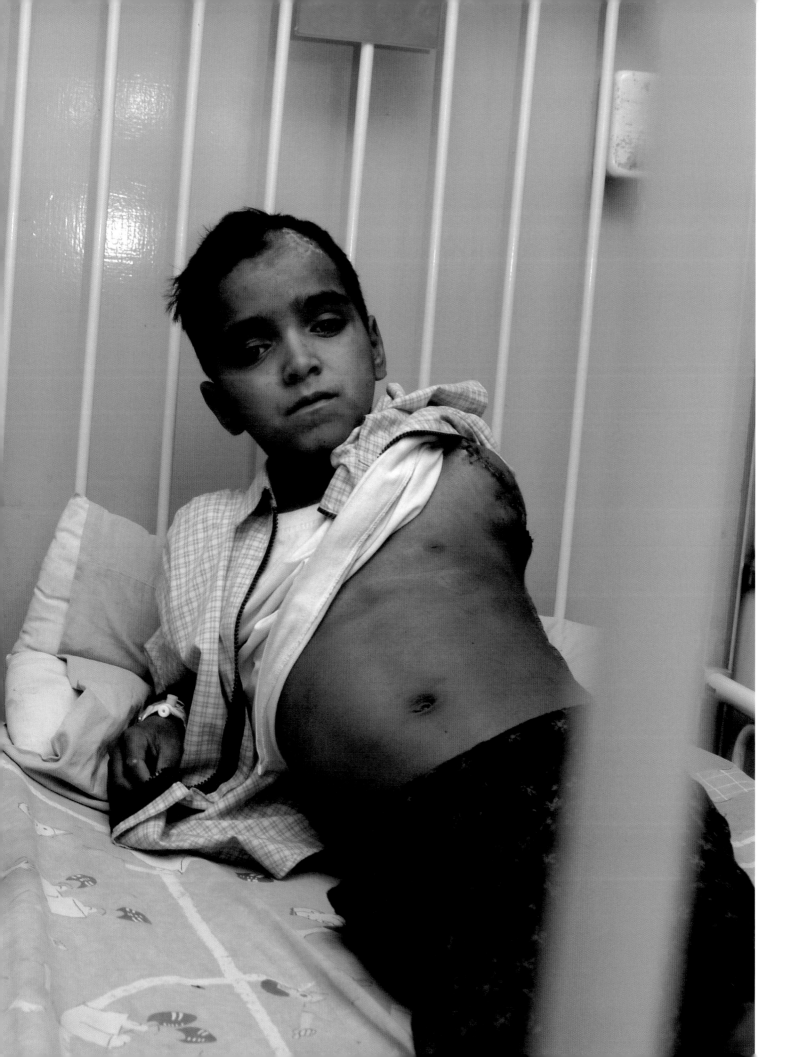

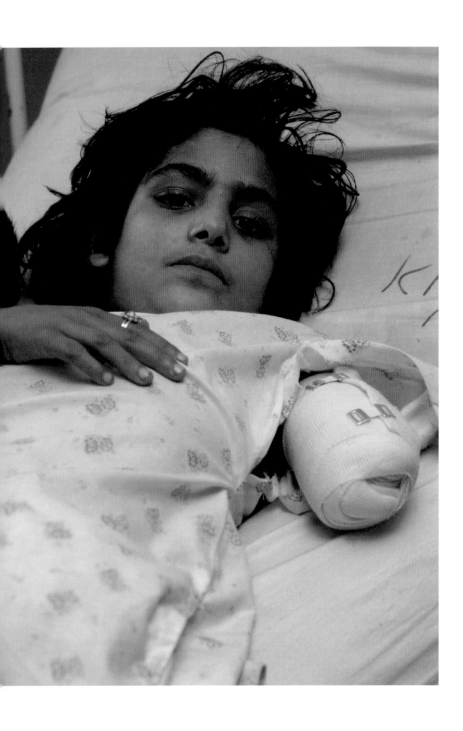

A young girl looks on after having her arm amputated at
the Pakistan Institute of Medical Sciences. Sohail Anjum

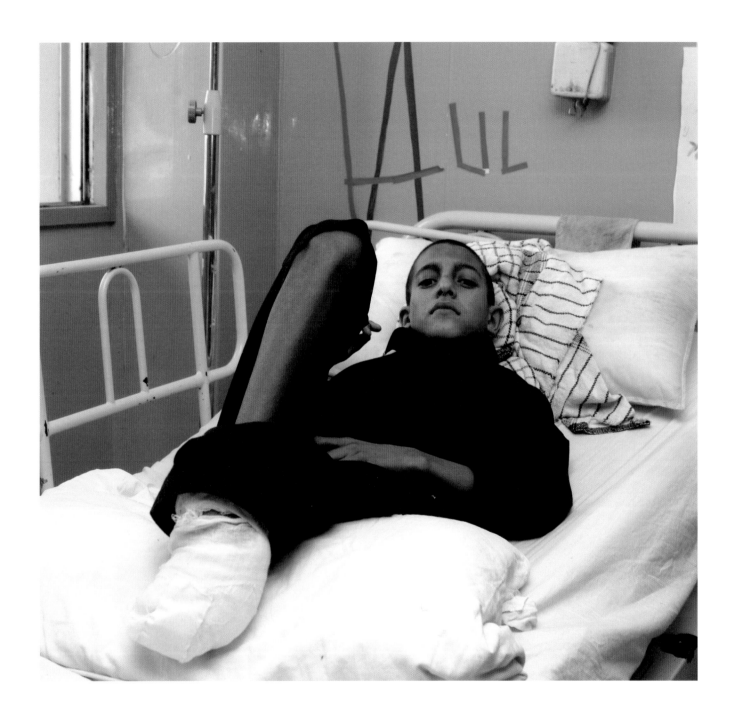

A young boy resting in the children's ward for the survivors of the earthquake at the Pakistan Institute of Medical Sciences. Sohail Anjum

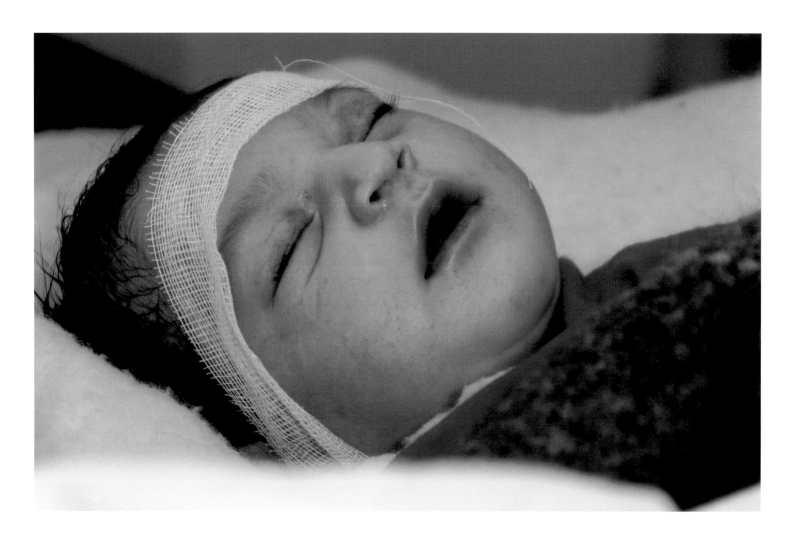

Start of a new life: A new born baby, born just six days after the
earthquake, sleeps at INOR Hospital, Abbotabad. Sohail Anjum

A young baby sleeps after receiving medical treatment in the children's
ward of the Pakistan Institute of Medical Sciences. Sohail Anjum

Left: A young baby recovers from leg fractures in the children's ward for survivors of the earthquake at the Pakistan Institute of Medical Sciences. Sohail Anjum

Right: A father bottle-feeds his young son, recovering from fractures to his legs at the Pakistan Institute of Medical Sciences. Sohail Anjum

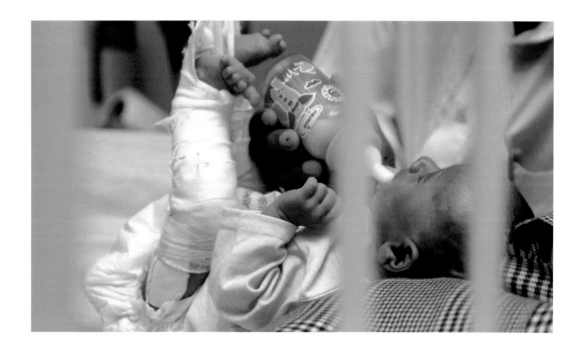

A young boy sits on his bed in the children's ward of the Pakistan Institute of Medical Sciences. Sohail Anjum

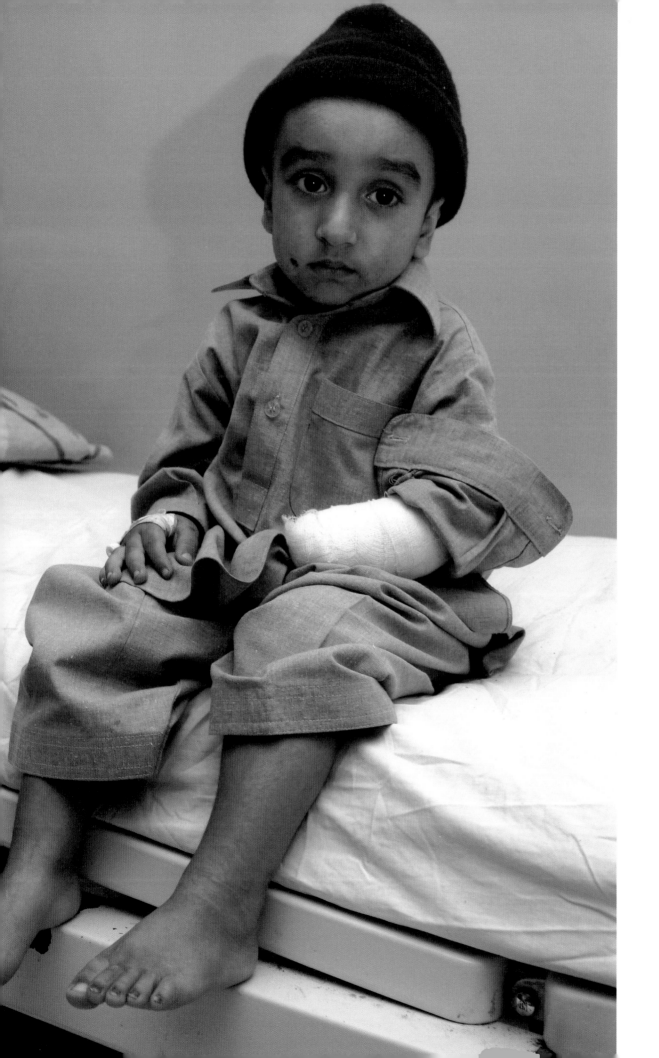

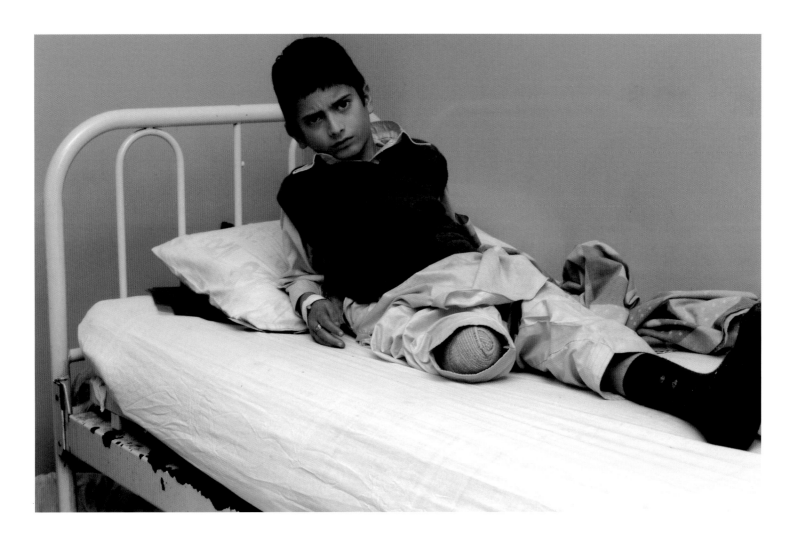

A teenage boy recovers in the children's ward of the
Pakistan Institute of Medical Sciences after having his
leg amputated. Sohail Anjum

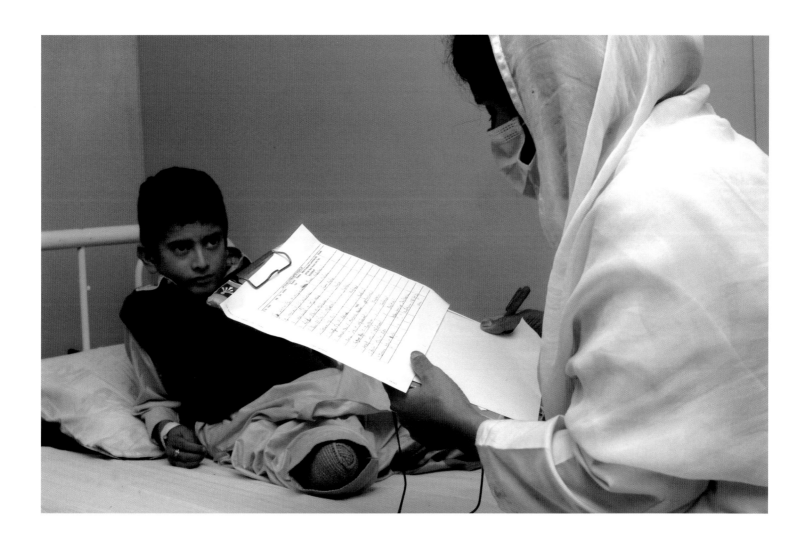

A member of the nursing staff attends to the boy following his operation. Sohail Anjum.

Next page: A young child lies unconscious in the children's ward for the survivors of the earthquake at the Pakistan Institute of Medical Sciences. Sohail Anjum

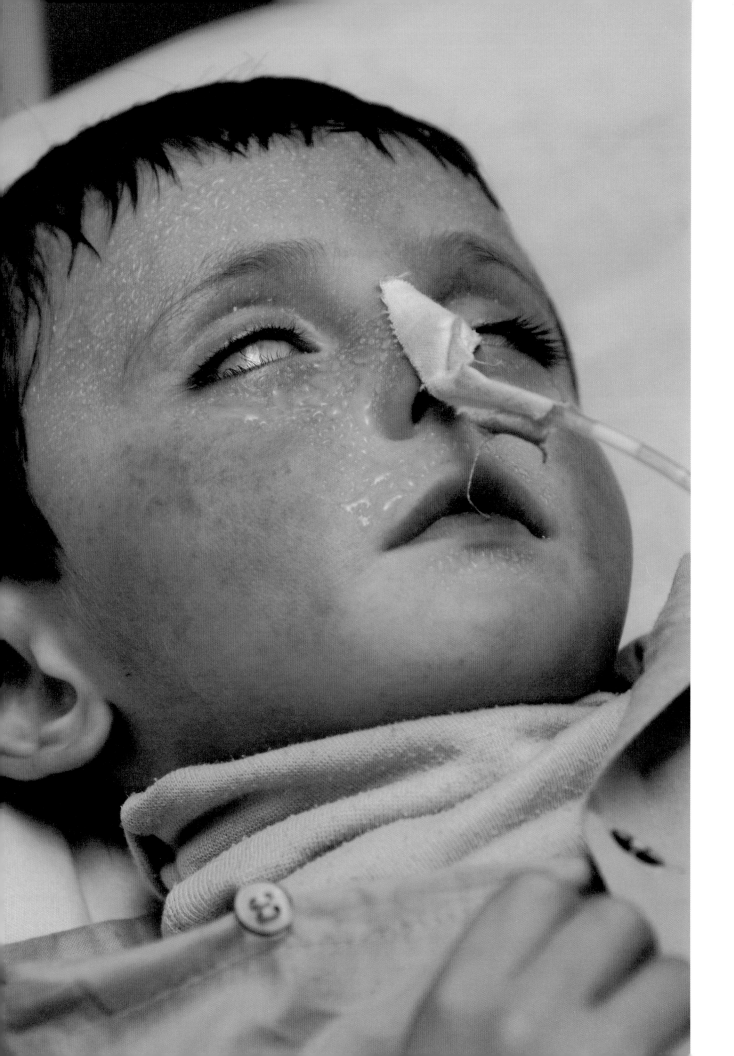

Necessities like ambulances, x-ray machines and scanning facilities exist only on paper. Many hospitals and basic medical health units do not have essential staff.

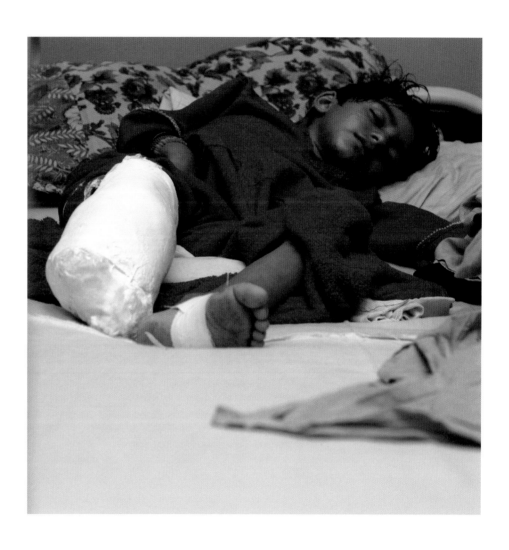

Left: A young boy recovers from multiple fractures
at the Al-Shifa Hospital in Rawalpindi. Sohail Anjum

Above: A young girl lies in bed at the Pakistan Institute
of Medical Sciences in Islamabad after a leg amputation
operation. Sohail Anjum

A mother cradles her young child who is recovering from a leg amputation in the children's ward of the Pakistan Institute of Medical Sciences in Islamabad. Sohail Anjum

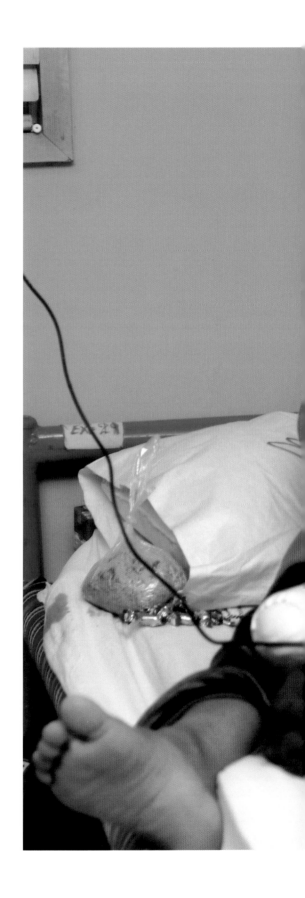

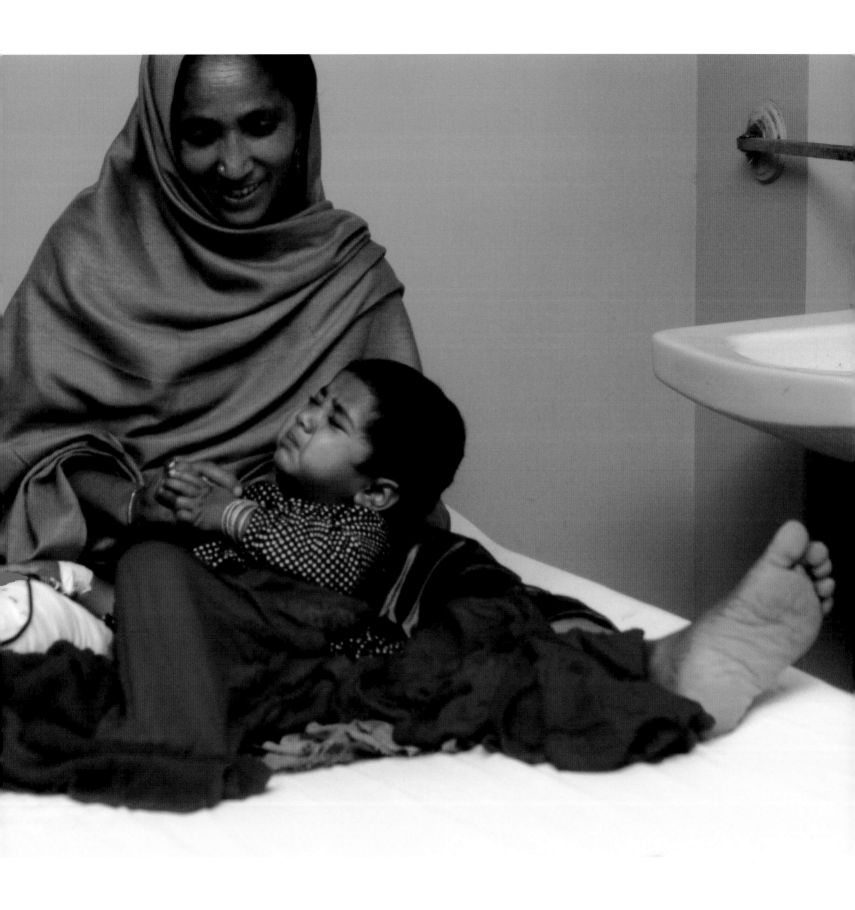

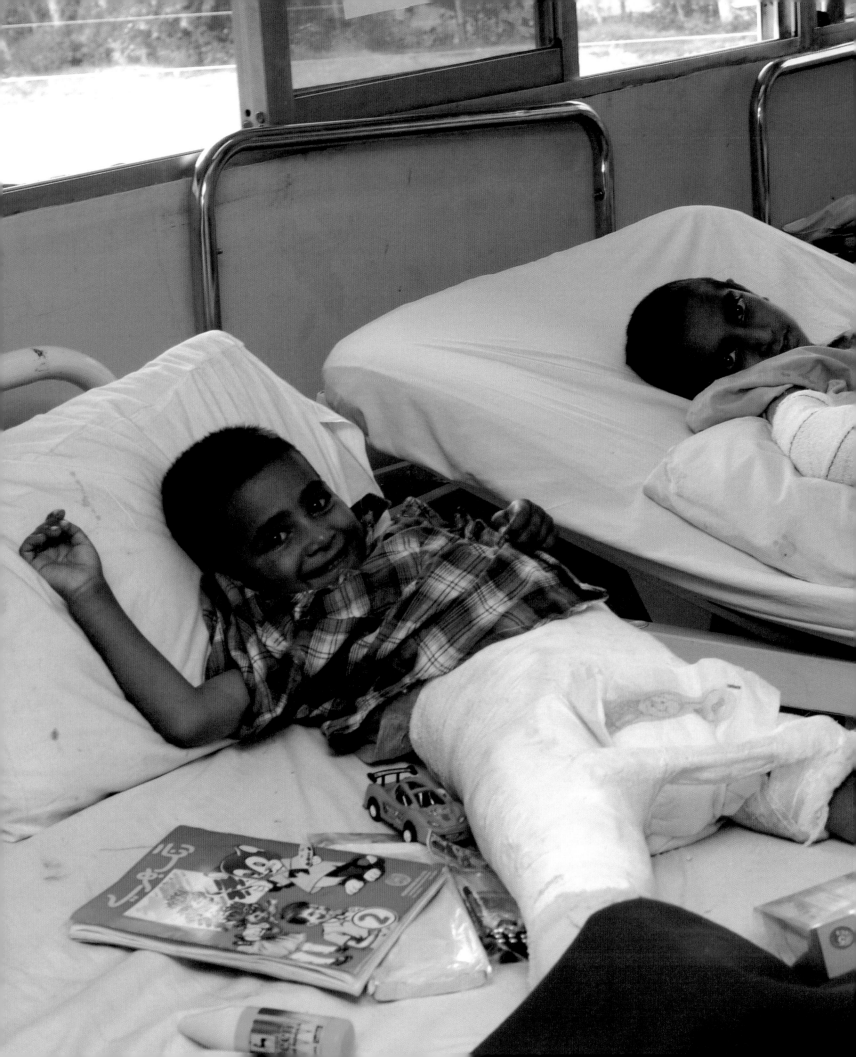

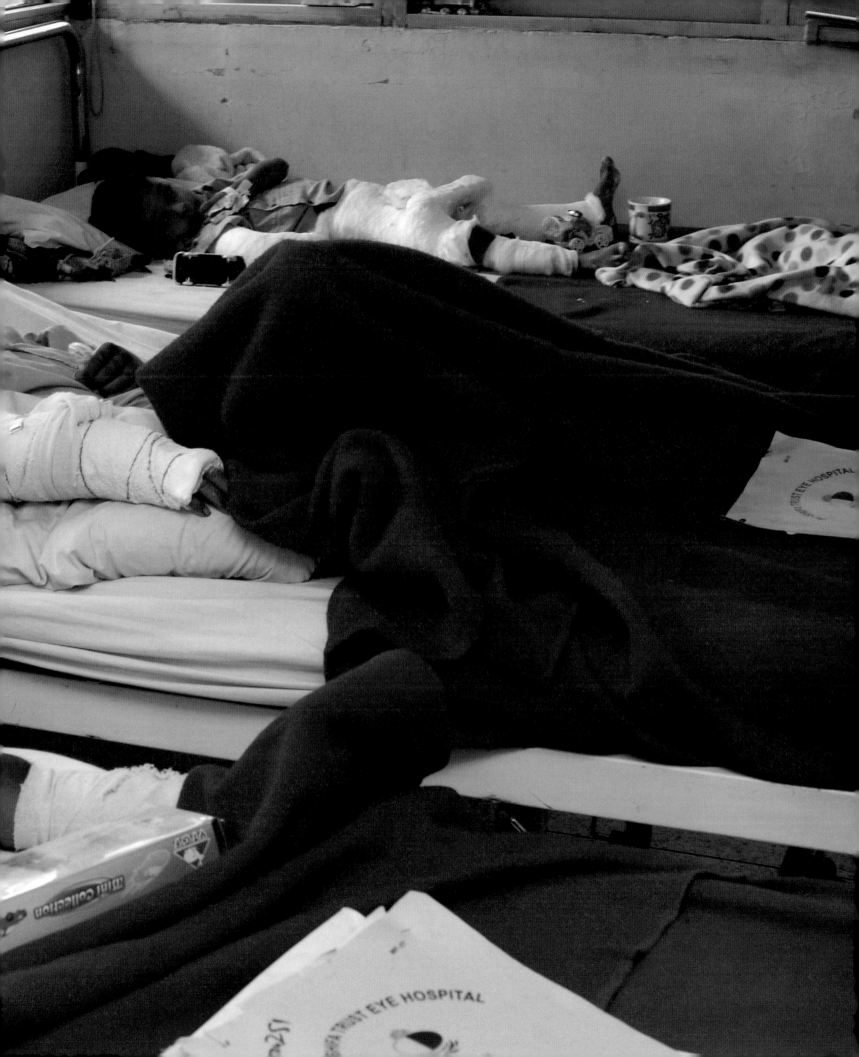

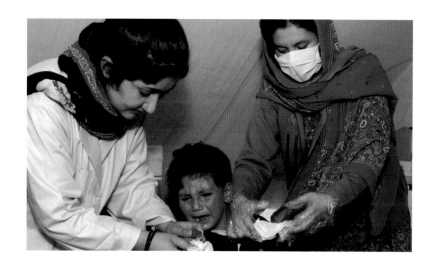

Previous page: Children recovering from fractures in a ward specially opened for survivors at Al-Shifa Hospital in Rawalpindi. Sohail Anjum

Left: A young boy looks through his hospital bed at the Pakistan Institute of Medical Sciences in Islamabad. Sohail Anjum

Above: The medical staff at the Aga Khan Health Service camp attend to an injured child in Muzaffarabad. Sohail Anjum

A young boy recovers from a fractured arm
at Al-Shifa Hospital in Rawalpindi. Sohail Anjum

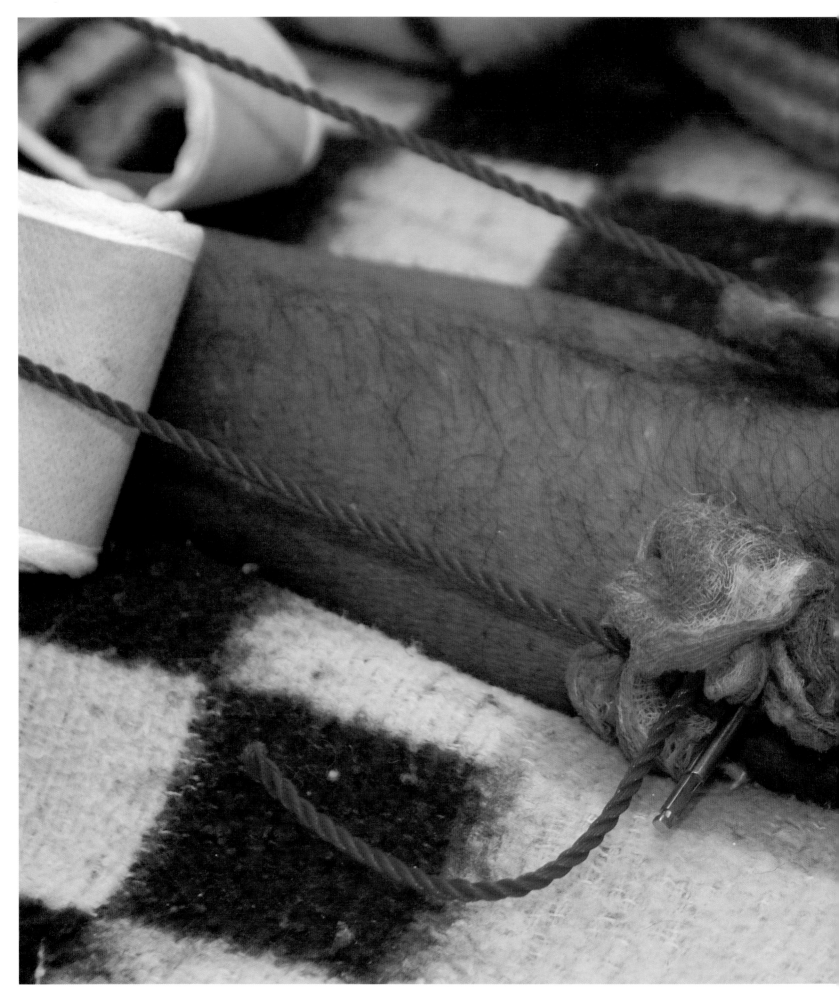

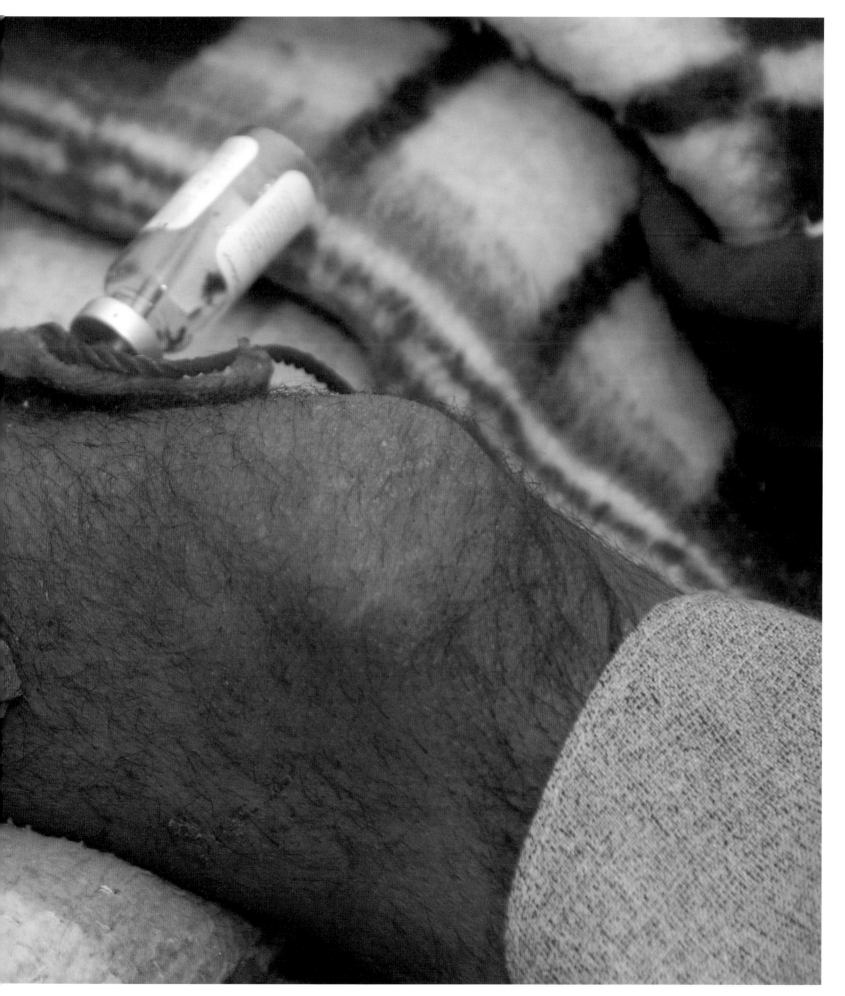

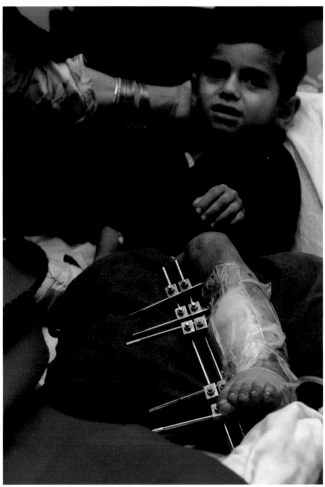

Previous page: A patient awaits a leg amputation at INOR Hospital, Abbotabad. Sohail Anjum

Above: A young girl examines her hands as she recovers from leg burns in the children's ward of the Pakistan Institute of Medical Sciences in Islamabad. Sohail Anjum

Above right: A mother soothes her young son as he recovers from his injuries at the Combined Military Hospital in Rawalpindi. Sohail Anjum

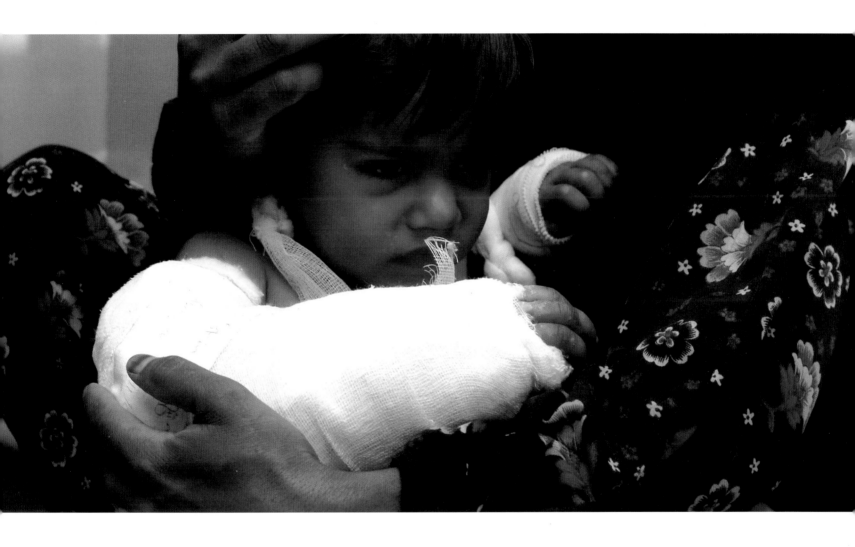

Above: A mother cradles her young child, recovering from fractures to the arms in the children's ward of the Pakistan Institute of Medical Sciences in Islamabad. Sohail Anjum

Next page: Kinza Pervaiz recovers from an arm amputaion in a relief camp established by the British charity, Helping Hands Worldwide, within the grounds of the Ayub Medical College Hospital in Abbotabad. Sohail Anjum

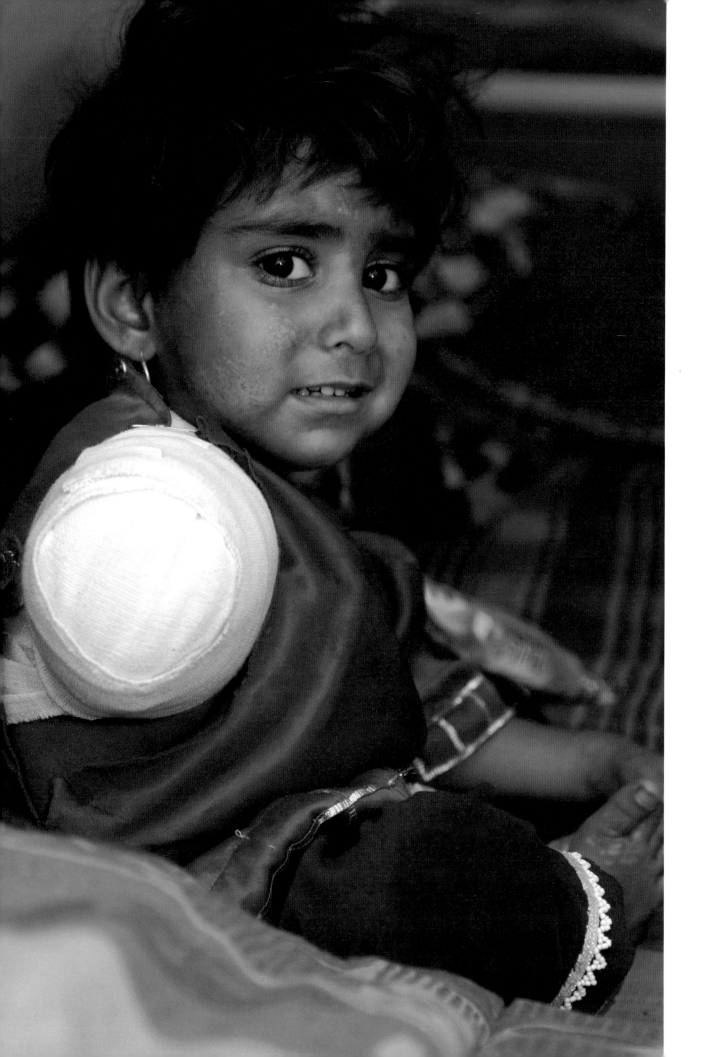

'We were all hoping to be engineers and doctors, but now we can't even think about our futures. We have nothing left.'

Above: An elderly woman mourns the death of her relatives at their graves in Neelum Valley. Getty Images

Right: A Kashmiri survivor looking lost at a relief camp in Abbotabad. Sohail Anjum

An injured woman with tears in her eyes sits in shock waiting to be evacuated from Balakot. *Getty Images*

Two days after the quake, a Pakistani woman cradles her injured granddaughter while waiting for rescue along with thousands of other residents in the completely destroyed town of Balakot. Getty Images

147

Left: A young child living in one of the makeshift camps on the outskirts of Balakot. Sohail Anjum

Centre: Brothers in arms: Two young survivors take time out to pose for the camera at a camp near Bagh. Sohail Anjum

Right: Looking into the future? A young Kashmiri boy looks on while others are busy playing. Sohail Anjum

Far right: Just one of the thousands of children who have been left homeless by the earthquake and are now living in makeshift camps. Sohail Anjum

Above: Thousands of children were affected by the earthquake. Many lost parents, while others were seriously hurt. The Pakistani media was full of suggestions about the future of those who had been orphaned but the government has decided that these children will only be offered for adoption by close relatives or the state will take care of them.
Sohail Anjum

Right: Children will be children: Young survivors playing at a relief camp in Bagh. Sohail Anjum

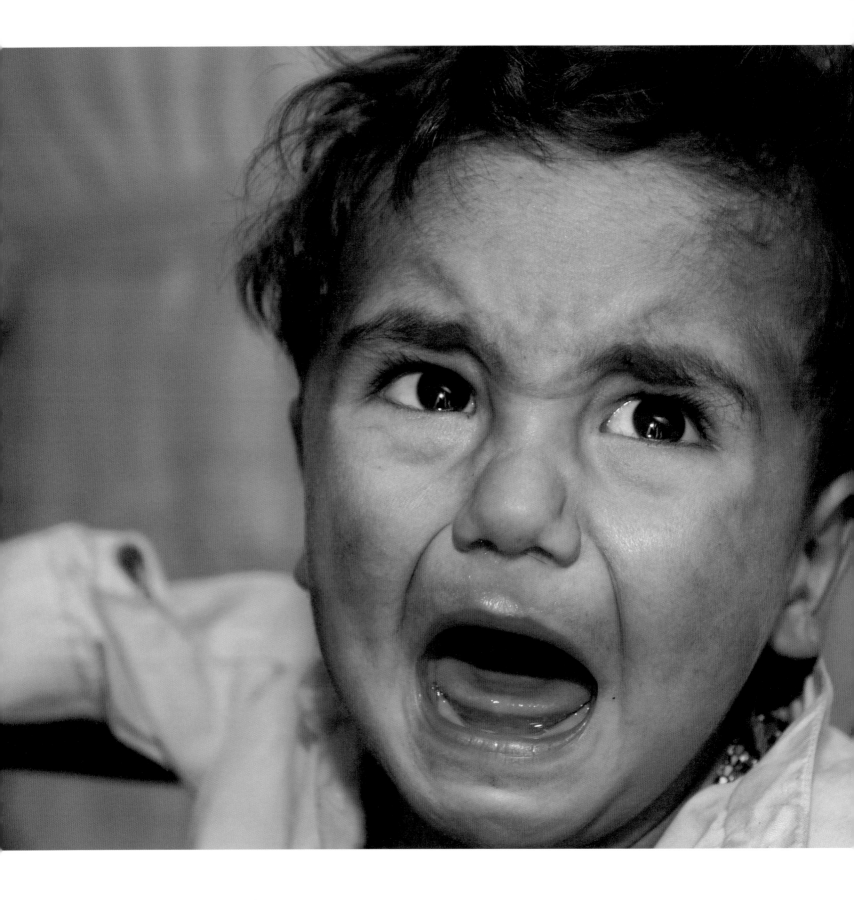

A young boy cries as he receives medical attention
in the Aga Khan Health Service camp in Muzaffarabad.
Sohail Anjum

Above: Many of the patients brought to the makeshift medical camps had serious injuries. Twenty-year-old Bibi Murhaba, with a fractured spine, was one of them. She underwent emergency treatment at a relief camp established within the grounds of Ayub Medical College Hospital in Abbotabad. Sohail Anjum

Right: Six-year-old Hussain Shah resting at a tented village in Abbotabad. Sohail Anjum

Above: An Indian Kashmiri child cries in Drangyari, some 80 miles northwest of Srinagar. Getty Images

Right: A young Kashmiri girl poses for the camera while her family prepares for the evening meal in a camp for survivors near Bagh. Sohail Anjum

Left: A young girl sits in the rubble after her family home in Balakot was destroyed. Sohail Anjum

Above: A young Kashmiri girl contemplates her situation as life starts to settle in a relief camp in Bagh. Sohail Anjum

A survivor, Rabel, attends a programme in celebration of
'World Children's Day', in Muzaffarabad almost six weeks
after the quake. Getty Images

People wandered around aimlessly, they were desperate for help but wouldn't ask. They didn't want to lose their self-respect.

Guarding the unguardable: A young boy stands in a collapsed building in Bagh.
Sohail Anjum

Previous page: A survivor left homeless and bereaved.
Panos Pictures

Above: An old Kashmiri woman arrives at a relief camp
in Abbotabad. Sohail Anjum

Right: An elderly Pakistani Kashmiri woman in pain
in a Muzaffarabad hospital. Sohail Anjum

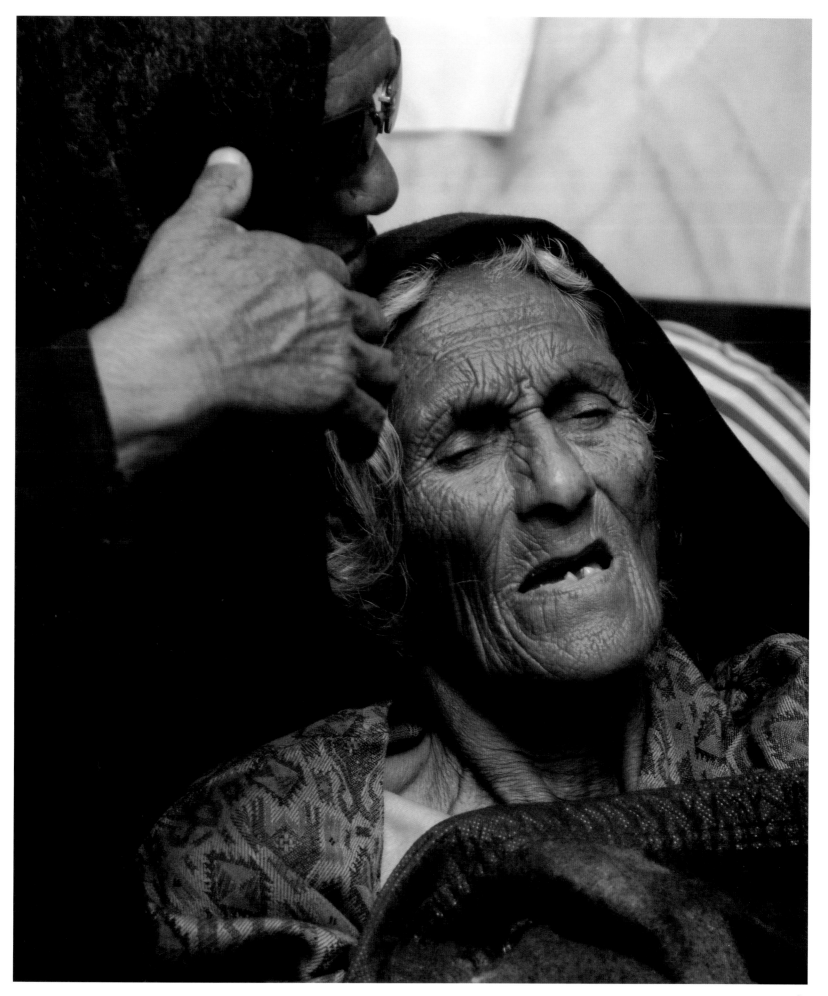

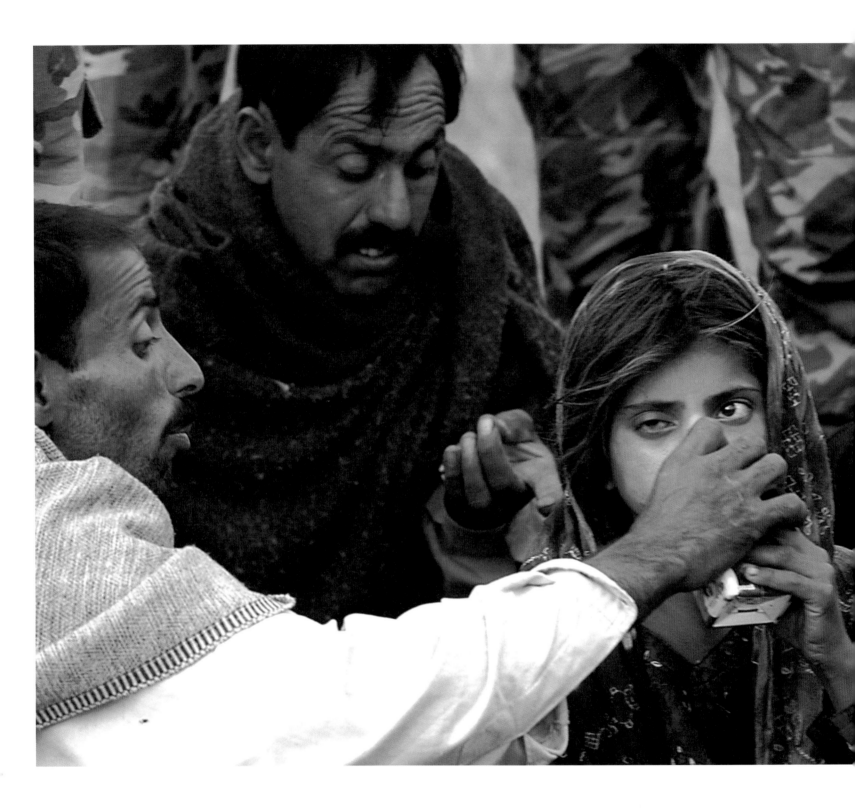

Family members tend to injured children. They were flown by helicopter to Chaklala military air base from their destroyed village near the Line of Control. *Panos Pictures*

A Pakistani woman waits to meet visiting US President George W Bush at the Presidential House in Islamabad on 4 March, 2006. *Getty Images*

Left: Life goes on: a little boy plays with a toy car amidst the rubble of his family home in Balakot. Sohail Anjum

Above: Kashmiri survivors scramble for a carton of milk at a makeshift relief camp in the midst of a devastated residential area of Muzaffarabad. Pakistan battled huge odds to deliver aid to hungry and traumatised people in the weeks after the disaster. Getty Images

Unknown future: A young man sits amidst
the wreckage of a collapsed building in Balakot.
Sohail Anjum

A Kashmiri family takes refuge at a tented village in Bagh. The village, raised by the British charity Helping Hands Worldwide, consists of 36 tents, each one to house a family of between four and eight people. Other international charities also provided daily provisions and medical care to many in the disaster-hit areas. Sohail Anjum

Injured Pakistani Kashmiri survivors exchange Eid greetings
in Muzaffarabad. Getty Images

A lost life: An old man sits in despair amongst
the collapsed buildings of Balakot. Sohail Anjum

Volunteers bury bodies in a mass grave in Balakot. Those who shared lives together for years didn't know they would one day share a grave. Getty Images

No time for festivities. On Eid ul-Fitr, two Kashmiri quake surviving women mourn over a family grave in Muzaffarabad. Getty Images

Those gone will always be remembered. Getty Images

From international charities to Muslim relief organisations and from Islamist groups to Kashmiri liberationists, all were running camps for the victims.

Left: 12 November, 2005 – Pakistani Army officer Shahid (top) and Indian Army officer J Nair meet on a footbridge connecting Indian-administered Kashmir and Pakistan-administered Kashmir during a relief exchange in Teetwal, 120 miles west of Srinagar. India and Pakistan opened a third crossing point on the disputed Kashmir border to help aid get to desperate earthquake survivors as fresh rain and snow hit the Himalayan region. Getty Images

Centre: Pakistani Lt Colonel Basit Shuja (L) shakes hands with Indian Colonel Gyan Misra on 16 November, 2005, prior to the opening of the fifth crossing point for aid supplies on the Line of Control (LoC) in Hajipir Uri. Getty Images

Right: Indian Kashmiri residents cross the Line of Control near the damaged Kaman Bridge on 17 November, 2005. Getty Images

Above: A Pakistani girl cries before getting her tetanus and measles vaccination at the US Mobile Army Surgical Hospital. Getty Images

Right: A billboard in Balakot shows Pakistani President Musharraf promising full reconstruction of the devastated areas. Sohail Anjum

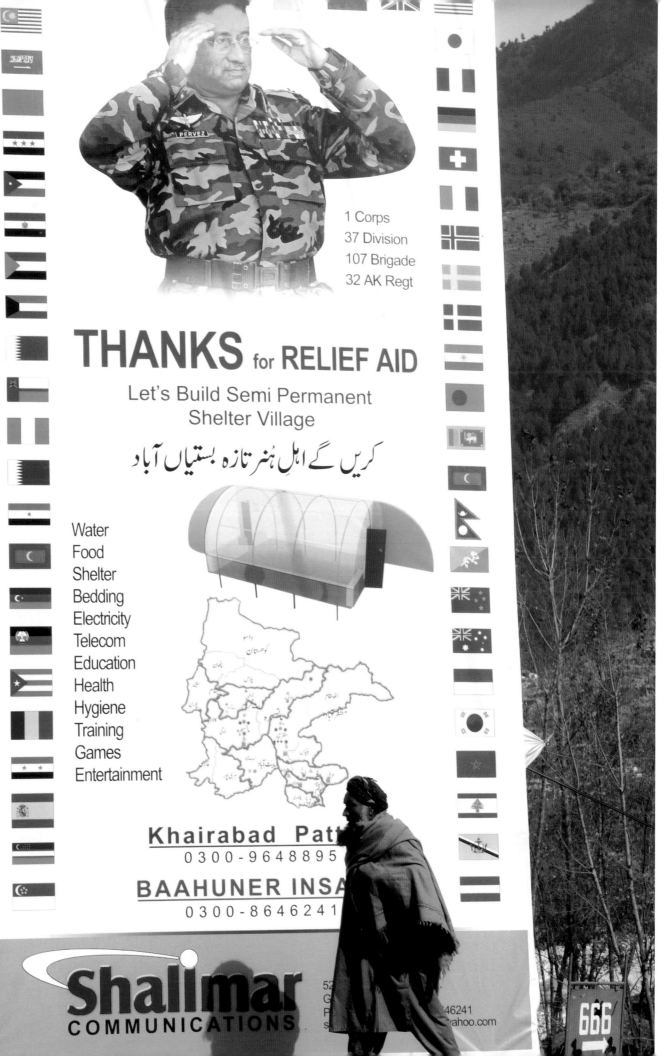

Pakistani villagers, from Jura in the Neelum Valley, look on through barbed wire as bags of wheat from USAID are dropped off by a WFP helicopter. *Getty Images*

A month after the disaster, people are still looking for
relatives amongst the photographs of injured victims
on a board outside a hospital in Peshawar. Getty Images

Graffiti in Balakot demanding that British Prime Minister
Tony Blair pull his medical team out of Pakistan. Solhail Anjum

Previous page: Unwanted aid: Thousands of donated clothes litter a Balakot street. Despite the donors best intentions some aid items were simply inappropriate. Solhail Anjum

Left: 7 November, 2005 – Pakistani policemen baton charge and fire tear-gas on Kashmiri demonstrators trying to cross the Line of Control at Titrinote, following its opening for earthquake relief. Getty Images

Centre: Hide and seek goes on between Pakistani policemen and Kashmiri demonstrators trying to cross the Line of Control. Getty Images

Right: A Pakistani policeman intercepts a man and his child as they try to cross the Line of Control at Titrinote. Getty Images

Left: Muzaffarabad: Pakistani Kashmiri students walk to school in
a camp for people made homeless by the earthquake. Getty Images

Right: A tented camp for displaced people. In the background is the
rubble of what used to be the thriving town of Balakot. Panos Pictures

No more games: The International Committee of Red Cross takes over the cricket ground in Muzaffarabad to set up a tent village to treat the wounded. Solhail Anjum

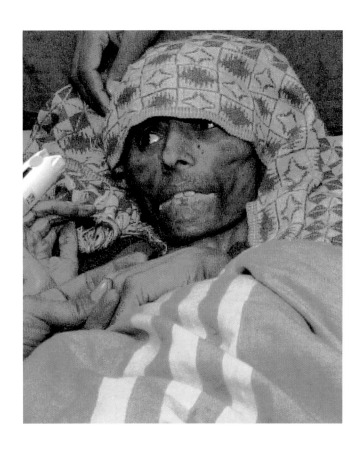

Pakistani paramedics treat Naqsha, a Kashmiri survivor, in an intensive care unit of a hospital in Muzaffarabad. Naqsha, in her 40s, was rescued from the rubble of her home 64 days after being buried by the earthquake.
Getty Images

The UN warned of a second wave of deaths if international aid pledges did not arrive in time.

President Pervez Musharraf and UN Secretary General Kofi Annan visited
a camp for survivors in Muzaffarabad on 18 November, 2005. The visit
was a day ahead of a donor conference in Islamabad. Getty Images

A bevy of international personalities visited the devastated areas – presidents, prime ministers, princes and princesses, politicians and Hollywood celebrities. All good public relations, but what did the people gain from it? Mostly nothing at all.

6 March, 2006: Pakistani Prime Minister Shaukat Aziz and British Prime Minister Tony Blair meet with members of the British military and emergency workers who helped survivors of the disaster. Getty Images

Norwegian Prime Minister Jens Stoltenberg playing with children at a UNICEF Health Centre during a visit to Garhi Habibullah on 6 December, 2005. Getty Images

The Archbishop of Canterbury, Rowan Williams (L) and Pakistani Religious
Minister Ejaz-ul-Haq pose for photographers at Jamia Manzoor-ul-Islamia,
a Pakistani Islamic seminary in Lahore on 26 November, 2005. Williams was
in Pakistan to see the aftermath of the disaster. Getty Images

Indian Bollywood film-star Manisha Koirala arrived in Pakistan
on a one-day visit to participate in the Pakistani-based television
programme 'Pukar' for the earthquake victims. Getty Images

Australian Prime Minister John Howard meets school children in an
Australian Defence Force health care centre during his visit to Dhanni,
in the earthquake-affected region on the Pakistan side of the Line Of
Control on 24 November, 2005. Getty Images

Australian Prime Minister John Howard enjoys a game of cricket with Australian and Pakistani troops and locals of Dhanni during his visit to the earthquake-affected region. Getty Images

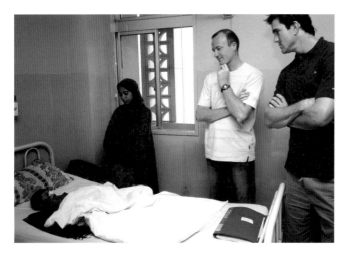

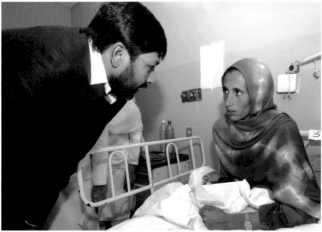

Top: England cricket team members Sean Udal (L) and Kevin Pietersen tour a children's ward for survivors of the earthquake at the Pakistan Institute of Medical Sciences on 29 October, 2005 in Islamabad, Pakistan. Getty Images

Bottom: Pakistan cricket captain Inzamam-ul Haq talks with the mother of an injured survivor at the Pakistan Institute of Medical Sciences hospital in Islamabad on 30 October, 2005. Getty Images

26 November, 2005 – Hollywood heart throb and UNHCR Goodwill Ambassador Angelina Jolie listens as a woman in Jabel Sharoon village, 2,000 metres above sea level in Pakistan-administered Kashmir, tells a UNHCR worker about her preparations for the coming winter. Getty Images

Jordan's Queen Rania (L) shakes hands with a survivor at the Abbas Hospital during her visit to the devastated city of Muzaffarabad on 29 October, 2005. The Queen visited the capital as a representative of the United Nations Children's Fund (UNICEF), bringing a plane load of relief supplies with her. Getty Images

President Pervez Musharraf arrives at the Donor's Conference in Islamabad, 19 November, 2005. International donors pledged over $6b for Pakistan to recover from the earthquake's devastation. Many in Pakistan believed these pledges would remain unfulfilled. Getty Images

Left: Former US President and UN Special Envoy for Pakistan Earthquake Relief, George H W Bush holds a Pakistani boy during his visit to a relief camp in Islamabad on 17 January, 2006. Getty Images

Centre: United States Senator and former Democratic Presidential candidate John Kerry presents a new school dress to a young girl during his visit to the Mehra camp in Shangla, a town in North West Frontier Province, on 14 January, 2006. Getty Images

Right: US President George W Bush talks with Pakistani earthquake survivors, as US First Lady Laura Bush and Pakistani First Lady Sehba Musharraf look on, at the Presidential House in Islamabad on 4 March, 2006. Getty Images

Left: Pakistani cricket hero Imran Khan, Kashmiri freedom fighter Yasin Malik and Pakistan's Jamaat-e-Islami leader Qazi Hussain Ahmed join thousands of Kashmiri Muslims to celebrate the Eid festival in Muzaffarabad. Special prayers were said for those killed in the devastating earthquake. Getty Images

Right: 4 November, 2005 – The president of the Jammu Kashmir Liberation Front (JKLF) in Indian held-Kashmir Yasin Malik (C) and cricketer-turned politician Imran Khan (R) greet Kashmiri children on the first day of the religious festival of Eid al-Fitr in Muzaffarabad. Getty Images

British Muslim MPs (from left to right) Sadiq Khan,
Mohammad Sarwar and Shahid Malik visiting a relief
camp in Bagh. Sohail Anjum

'People were hospitable and wouldn't let me leave without having dinner with them. By tradition, a guest must not go without having a meal.'

An Edhi Foundation volunteer cuts a pipe for a shelter in Chala Bandi, some 3 miles from Muzaffarabad. The Foundation has initiated a project in the Kashmiri capital to manufacture 20,000 homes made from arched steel pipes and galvanised iron sheets. More than three million people were made homeless by the earthquake. Getty Images

Weeks after the earthquake, RAF Chinook rescue helicopters,
part of the Pakistan earthquake relief party, are still busy in the
skies over Islamabad. Getty Images

Far left: A Kashmiri girl stands outside her temporary home in a tented village outside the devastated city of Muzaffarabad. Getty Images

Above left: A man prepares to cook a chapatti on a makeshift stove set up amid the debris of his destroyed house. Sohail Anjum

Above right: Daily life resumes for this shopkeeper four weeks after the earthquake destroyed most of Balakot. Sohail Anjum

Bottom right: A ruse to relieve reality – children play cricket in a tented village for people made homeless by the earthquake outside Muzaffarabad. Getty Images

Left: Children will always be children. Getty Images

Above: Happiness cutting through horror – Kashmiri bride Abida Bibi displays her henna tattoos during her wedding ceremony at a refugee camp. Getty Images

Left: Back in business – roadside shops selling fruit and vegetables reopen in Muzaffarabad. Getty Images

Right: A young Pathan vegetable vendor faces the reality that many of his previously regular customers will not be returning to his stall. Sohail Anjum

A young girl, displaced by the earthquake, living in one of the fast-expanding tent cities that have sprung up all over northern Pakistan.
Panos Pictures

Left: Myra performs during a programme to mark
'World Children's Day', in Muzaffarabad. Getty Images
Right: The healing power of laughter. Getty Images

Above: A young girl manages a smile despite her family home in the town of Balakot being destroyed. Sohail Anjum

Right: Two young girls pose for the camera near Balakot. Sohail Anjum

Next page: A girl displaced by the earthquake. Panos Pictures

'The government is one of the fatalities of the earthquake. There is no-one to talk to, nowhere to go to seek help.'

Survivors negotiate a land slide in the Neelum Valley. *Getty Images*

A Pakistani army bulldozer clears a landslide in the village of Peer Chanasi, some
15 miles from Muzaffarabad, seven weeks after the earthquake. Getty Images

A Kashmiri man struggles with a bundle of valuable fire wood near Muzaffarabad. International aid agencies continually warned that unless aid was received quickly thousands would be at risk as winter set in. Getty Images

Pakistani Kashmiri NGO workers trying to make sense of the chaos in a tented village constructed by Turkish workers near Muzaffarabad. Getty Images

Children run to collect urgent relief supplies dropped by helicopter in the Neelum Valley on 5 January, 2005. Helicopters resumed relief flights in the area following three days of heavy rain and snow, as authorities said many survivors were descending from the mountains. Getty Images

An Indian Kashmiri woman fights her way through the snow with firewood on a cold December day in Drangyari, 80 miles northwest of Srinagar. The October earthquake killed more 1,300 in India too. Getty Images

Three months after the earthquake, many survivors faced the harsh Himalayan winter in tents, like these donated by a relief organisation in Kandia. *Getty Images*

Houses spared by the earthquake stand amid snow-covered terrace fields near Batian, a little village in a mountainous area of northern Pakistan. Getty Images

Aamir Ghauri

Aamir Ghauri has travelled to the devastated areas three times since October 2005. First to see for himself the level of destruction and later to experience the Herculean efforts of the local people to start their lives afresh.

He feels that the October earthquake has demolished parts of his cherished memories 'Kashmir and the Northern Areas were my family's natural hideaway in Pakistan's sizzling summers. I find it difficult to recollect those memories without the images of death and devastation'.

Aamir Ghauri is the European Head of News and Current Affairs for Pakistan's Geo TV. Before joining Geo in March 2005, he worked for both the Pakistani and international media, including the BBC.

Ghauri has an MSc in International Politics from the London University's School of Oriental and African Studies. He also briefly practised law in Pakistan but left it for journalism in the late 1980s.

He was born in Pakistan but now lives in London with his wife *Fustina* and three children, *Omar, Ali* and *Asr*. Apart from his family, his other loves include travelling, people, books and movies.

Sohail Anjum

Like millions in Britain, Sohail Anjum was shocked to see the horrific TV images of the Pakistani earthquake. When offered a chance to travel to the quake-hit areas and be part of this project, his immediate reply was; 'When am I travelling?'

Within days of the earthquake, Anjum spent days travelling on perilous roads to once thriving towns of Abbotabad, Bagh, Balakot and Muzaffarabad in his attempt to record as much of the devastation as possible. Looking at tragedy and trauma was new to his lens, but a very valuable experience nonetheless.

A photographer by choice, London-born Anjum spends most of his time snapping celebrities for Britain's lifestyle magazines. But his biggest talent is the ease with which he is able to make the transition from one genre of photography to another.

His photographic work has featured in *Asiana, Eastern Eye, India Today, Libas*, and *Verve* magazine. He has also contributed to the *Evening Standard, News of the World and the Mail on Sunday*. Previously, he has worked as a Picture Editor for *Eastern Eye*.

Anjum likes to shoot on location and favours black and white photography.

Sponsors

Helping Hands is an international charitable organisation whose philosophy is humanism, whose objective is to serve humanity, and whose aim is to eradicate illiteracy, human suffering, poverty, disease and discrimination.

Islamic Relief is an international relief and development charity, which aims to alleviate the suffering of the world's poorest people. It is an independent Non-Governmental Organisation founded in the UK in 1984.

British Telecom provides information and applications where they are needed in a networked world, through an extensive range of voice, data, fixed, wireless and mobile solutions. BT has over 30,000 people around the world providing service in 170 countries.

Bestway Group is the second largest cash and carry group in the United Kingdom. Founded by Sir Anwar Pervez OBE, H Pk, more than 40 years ago, the group is also respected for its humanitarian and charitable contributions both in the UK and overseas.

NetSol Technologies, Inc. designs, develops, markets and exports software products to customers in the automobile, finance, leasing and banking industries worldwide. It also provides a consulting service and cost-effective development of customised application software.

Hamilton Bradshaw is an international private equity investment firm that focuses on Venture Capital, Buyouts, and Management/Institutional Buyouts. Our team includes successful entrepreneurs and established investment professionals and they seek meaningful investments in companies where operating management will have a significant holding and we support expansion and development.

HAMILTON BRADSHAW

Acknowledgments

Incessant phone calls woke me up at about five in the morning on 8 October, 2005. The callers were barely known to me. But they were regular viewers of the Pakistani satellite TV channel for which I work. They were all British Pakistanis of Kashmiri origin, desperate for details of the earthquake that had just hit northern Pakistan and Kashmir. The calls did not stop for days and rightly so because Pakistan and Kashmir had never before experienced such a natural calamity.

I travelled to the disaster zone a few weeks later to see for myself what I had been hearing of – the unprecedented death toll, the government's confusion and inability to handle the post-quake crisis, tales of corruption, of the rescue and relief effort, stories of miraculous escapes and more. It was a painful expedition, in fact, a *via dolorosa*, as the pain and human misery was unfathomable.

It was there that I thought of making a permanent record of my personal experience. My first thanks are to Mohammed Ashfaq Khan of Helping Hands, who immediately agreed to be a partner in the endeavour. I also want to thank Sohail Anjum, a friend for over a decade, for agreeing to swap his celebrity photographic circuit for documenting pain and suffering. This book is primarily a journey to the quake-hit areas through his lens. Since Anjum didn't arrive in Muzaffarabad until a few days after the earthquake, photographs acquired from Getty Images and Panos Pictures fill the short time gap.

My special thanks to Sajjad Nizam Shawl, Bilal Shafi Ghauri, Waseem Yaqoob, Adil Hussaini, Paul Falkner, Sir Anwar Pervez, Muzaffar Chaudhry, Kausar Kazmi, Naeem Ghauri, Najeeb Ghauri, James Caan, Lt Col Aijaz Akram, Dr Hanif S Esmail, Abdul Qayyum and to all those who wanted to remain unnamed despite their very valuable contribution to this book. I also want to thank Clare Playne and her team at Playne Design who made this project their own right from the start.

And how can I not thank my wife, Fustina, and our children Omar, Ali and Asr who understood my pain and persevered with me throughout this project.

Nine months on, the earthquake affected areas remain in dire need of the help that was promised to them by the Pakistani government and the international community. I hope this book will act as a reminder for those whose promises as yet remain unfulfilled.

Aamir Ghauri, 6 June, 2006, London

Credits

Published by Xenos UK Ltd, 2006

Xenos UK Ltd, 53 Selwood Road, Shirley Park,
Croydon CR0 7JU, United Kingdom
www.xenosuk.com

Text by Aamir Ghauri

Photographs by © Sohail Anjum, Getty Images and Panos Pictures
Portrait photographs by Theo Cohen

Editors: Gill Davies, Jane McCarten

Design and layout by Playne Design Ltd, London
www.playnedesign.co.uk

Printed by The Cavendish Press Ltd in the United Kingdom

ISBN: 0-9553442-0-4
978-0-9553442-0-6